Dalaradia

Dalaradia
Kingdom of the Cruthin

Ian Adamson

First published by Pretani Press 1998
638 Springfield Road, Belfast BT12 7DY

A Ulidia Book

Typeset by Island Publications, Newtownabbey
Printed in Northern Ireland by The Universities Press (Belfast) Ltd

Paperback ISBN 0 948868 25 2
Hardback ISBN 0 948868 26 0

For my beloved wife Kerry

Acknowledgements

Special thanks are due to Michael Hall for research, editing and typesetting and to Rowel Friers for the frontispiece.

The author is also grateful to David Adamson, Ann Brown, David Campbell, Douglas Carson, Robin Charley, Jackie Hewitt, Nora McNairney, Deborah Phillips and Philip Robinson for their assistance in the preparation of the manuscript for publication.

He fully appreciates all the help given by his family, friends and scholars alike, although their opinions are not necessarily those held by the author.

And I'm yearning for the mists of Dalaradia
And I miss the Lagan river running slow.

Brian Ervine

Other books by Ian Adamson

The Cruthin
The Identity of Ulster
The Ulster People
1690: William and the Boyne

Contents

Cráeb Tulcha, the sacred tree, literally 'spreading branch', and inauguration stone of ancient Ulster. The tree was cut down by the Uí Neill in AD 1099. The site has been identified as Crew Hill (Crewhollage), near Glenavy.

A Sense of Continuity

A Belfast community worker once told me that whenever he was asked to take groups of foreign visitors around the 'community network', he always included, weather permitting, a visit to the Giant's Ring, the large circular prehistoric earthwork situated close to the southern outskirts of the city. He believed that doing so helped provide his visitors with 'space' in which to process the flood of information with which they were invariably bombarded during their busy schedule of community encounters. But he hoped they would gain more than just a temporary respite, as he explained:

> I always felt it was important to provide the visitors, even in a small way, with 'a sense of place'; to help them experience the very real presence our landscape exudes; even get a feel for the way some localities seem to be infused with the Past. My hope was that it would also provide them with a deeper insight into the intensity both communities here bring to their seemingly immutable quarrel. For our conflict is in many ways territorial, between two communities who each feel the same passionate belonging to this land, and yet who feel threatened by what they perceive as the other's exclusive claims over it.

The tragedy is that these perceived threats, notwithstanding the wrongs perpetrated by each community upon the other in the distant and not-so-distant past, are unwarranted. Both communities in Northern Ireland have an equal claim to 'belonging', as much because ultimately they are the *same* community. I believe that if the citizens of Northern Ireland can become fully aware of the extent of their interrelatedness, not just with each other but with all the peoples of these islands, then a symbiosis of their respective identities could be established which would provide a solid foundation for the peace they so much deserve.

I began writing this book when coming to the end of my term as Lord Mayor of Belfast. Hence, it seemed appropriate to direct the focus of the book, though not exclusively so, upon the history of that area of which the Belfast region was once a part – the ancient Cruthin kingdom of Dalaradia. The Giant's Ring therefore serves as a useful starting point for me too, for although its erection long predates the emergence of Dalaradia, the antiquity once lay within Dalaradia's borderland.

   Just as we can glean 'a sense of place' when in such locations, those who have a deeper understanding of our history often experience an equally strong sense of 'continuity'. And that is one ingredient I hope will emerge from these pages – a living thread of continuity with our past, a past which should be the treasured inheritance of all our citizens, irrespective of their present religious and political allegiances. As Sir Samuel Ferguson, poet and eminent Gaelic scholar, once pointed out, an appreciation of one's own history is important so that

> men may feel they are not come in the world strangers, but members of a family long planted in the land before them, owing reverence to the place and institutions of their forefathers, and by that common sentiment strengthening the social bond among one another.[1]

Although readers will hopefully find much that will be new to

them in this book, there is inevitably some duplication of ma.
which has appeared in my other titles. However, given ι
present search for peace in our land, and my belief that aι
awareness of our *shared* history and culture can play a positive
role in that search, a restatement of our common heritage surely
cannot go amiss. As Raoul Vaneigem wrote:

> A minute correction of the essential is more important
> than a hundred new accessories.[2]

As readers will also discover, this book is more than a 'political
history' of Dalaradia – it is also a celebration of the rich literary
heritage which has been intimately associated with it, a heritage
which remains largely unknown to today's public.

A Living Inheritance

The circular earthwork known as the Giant's Ring, with a megalithic burial chamber positioned dramatically in its centre, is but one of many antiquities which abound throughout Ireland. Dolmens, court cairns, passage graves, stone circles, standing stones, Ogham stones, earthworks, raths, crannogs, round towers, high crosses, churches, monastic settlements, abbeys, castles . . . dot our landscape as visible evidence of our past. No other European country is so endowed with such a wealth of antiquities. Perhaps Ireland's position at the edge of Europe has had something to do with that, perhaps it is because the land has not been ploughed up to anywhere near the same extent as on the European mainland.

The finest of the megalithic tombs are situated in the Boyne valley, and P A O Síocháin wrote of them:

> Viewed from south of the river, the hill range above the Boyne with its great monumental mounds makes dramatic and impressive impact, creating an immediate respect for the intellectual capacity and vision of the people who, in the prehistoric past, selected it as the site for the development of a megalithic culture in art and architecture that is forever without equal. On it, in course of time, they created a great Stone Age complex of megalithic structures that was one of the wonders of the ancient world.[3]

More importantly, these antiquities are not simply 'cold'

monuments made of stone and earth, somehow remote from this island's present inhabitants; they are a tangible link with the communities who laboured at their construction. This seems perfectly logical: why should we expect Ireland's human presence to be any less enduring that its antiquities? O Síocháin added: 'No longer can we look on these as cold stones from a long dead era. Warm hands once held and gave them meaning and purpose; touch them and you touch your past.' H J Fleure stressed the significance of such a linkage through time:

> The megaliths are not a matter of a vanished people
> and a forgotten civilisation; they belong to the core of
> our heritage as western Europeans.[4]

In the heart of the territory which was to become known to history as Dalaradia lies the valley of the Six Mile Water, running west to Lough Neagh at Antrim, and, like the Boyne valley, it too contains a cemetery of Neolithic passage tombs which extends for several miles.

Even when the Celts arrived in Ireland these megalithic burial sites retained too strong an influence over the lives of the indigenous people to be ignored. Accordingly, Celtic kings often selected such places as the location for their own seats of power. As Francis Byrne pointed out:

> There can be no doubt at all of the extraordinary
> continuity of tradition exemplified at sites such as
> Tara and Knowth. This is in itself a strong argument
> for the survival of large elements of the megalithic
> people and of their beliefs in Ireland under the later
> Celtic overlay.[5]

Nor were the Celts the last to experience the awe in which such sites were held by the local population, as geographer Estyn Evans discovered:

> It has more than once been my experience to be refused

permission to excavate megalithic monuments from the owner's belief that bad luck would follow. Country people will not touch the trees that grow on ancient burial sites, for instance they will not even use fallen branches as fuel.[6]

These megalithic sites, particularly the stone circles, were viewed well into modern times as the domain of the 'fairy-folk'; indeed, such beliefs persist even today. During the writing of this book a TV news item[7] reported that when building workers unknowingly disturbed a 'fairy ring' near Kilkeel in County Down three of them suffered separate accidents, serious enough to require hospitalisation. The other labourers could not be persuaded to continue with the work, and the object they had unintentionally erected in 'fairy territory' – an electricity kiosk – was eventually dismantled and the ground restored as best as possible to its former state. Two weeks later the *Irish News* carried a report[8] on workmen being similarly 'forced' off a building site near Buncrana, County Donegal, by the 'little people'. Country folk throughout Ireland could recount numerous such stories, and not always in a disbelieving manner.

I have no intention of entering into debate on the legitimacy or otherwise of such ancient belief. I merely wish to draw attention to its remarkable tenacity. The 'leave well alone' attitude which still surrounds megalithic sites throughout Ireland is merely one facet of the rich tapestry of folklore and superstition which accords an almost living presence to much of this island's landscape – from its mountains and streams to its wells and 'fairy thorns'.

W G Wood-Martin pointed out that those beliefs and customs now derided as 'quaint' or 'superstitious' must have sprung from the same questioning uncertainty which lies at the root of all religious belief:

Myths, and tales invented to teach a moral, remain at

the base of all thought and of all creeds, for legends endowed with apparent ever-enduring vitality, shadowy traditions of old-world life, echoes which vibrate in the folklore of every people, are embedded in scattered fragments in present-day faiths . . . Primitive rights, which have been banished for centuries from religion as publicly practised, are kept alive in local superstitions; for there has never been an epoch in the existence of any race in which all old institutions, all old ideas, have suddenly vanished, yielding place to a brand-new religion.[9]

These ancient beliefs and customs comprise an aspect of our inheritance towards which we should not feel dismissive; rather, it should be valued as an essential part of everything which makes us what we are today, a conclusion reached by Estyn Evans:

I became convinced that a significant factor in what is sometimes called the essential unity of Ireland . . . has been the retention, persisting in many areas into modern times, of certain attitudes towards the world and the otherworld, of traditional customs, beliefs and seasonal festivals which had often assumed the guise of Christian piety, but which had their origins in the Elder Faiths of pre-Christian times.[10]

As Evans indicates, nowhere is the continuity between old and new more evident than in the manner in which the 'Elder Faiths' interacted with Christianity, something also conceded by Cardinal Tomás Ó Fiaich:

The highly sophisticated designs which soon appear on the earliest stone crosses, manuscripts and metalwork were in the same tradition as those on the gold and bronze ornaments of pre-Christian Ireland. . . . Even the holy places and objects of pre-Christian

Ireland – the sacred wells and stones and trees – were incorporated into the Christian tradition. The festival of Lugh at the end of July was baptised by the thousands who later honoured St Patrick on the Reek. The pagan festival at the beginning of spring was replaced by St Brigid's Feast on 1 February. Even the heroes of the earlier tales were given a place in the Christian pantheon. For example King Conor Mac Nessa was made a contemporary of Christ and died in an attempt to defend him, and Oisín was brought back from Tír na n-Óg to be baptised by Patrick.[11]

All those things bequeathed us by our ancestors – from the magnificent megaliths and simple raths to the all-pervasive folklore – connect us to those forebears in some way. One musicologist remarked that it is 'inconceivable that all vestiges of the music that sustained our people for perhaps two thousand years could have vanished without trace.'[12] If so, then it is worth noting that Irish music is currently exporting this aspect of our ancient inheritance worldwide to increasing acclaim.

Such a connection with the world beyond these shores is nothing new. Nowhere is this better exemplified than in the rich wealth of folklore, much of it in the oral tradition, still lovingly preserved by the population. A study, published in 1963, listed the sheer abundance of international tales still being told throughout Ireland: it recorded nearly 43,000 tellings of over 900 international tales.[13] As Estyn Evans pointed out:

> In our own day, a rich vein of oral tradition has revitalised creative writing. The very poverty of the tattered ends of Europe has helped to preserve old values, to favour personal expression in poetry, oratory, music and song, where one man is as good as the next and all are independent of capital equipment, rather than in those arts requiring joint endeavour and a large investment . . . Thanks to such continuities,

Ireland has more than once been able to hand back to the outside world gifts which it received and enriched with its own genius.[10]

The vibrant oral tradition which sustained this vast repertoire has never been extinguished, as is evident in this description of a storyteller in action in the early 1930s:

He sat on the hob beside the fire to tell the story, his eyes fixed upon me like two awls. His body was swaying and his limbs trembling with the intensity of the telling. He raised his voice now and lowered it again, as would an actor on the stage. You might think that he belonged no more to this present world of ours, but had gone back to the ancient world of the heroes and was trying to make that world live in his story. All the characters in the tale were living people to him. Listening to him one realised how great was the old-world art of the storytellers.[14]

The rich inheritance of our ancient past, therefore, is not something remote from us, encased behind glass in museum displays, but a vital, 'living' component of the very personality of this island and its inhabitants.

Pre-Celts and Celts

Although the dolmens, court cairns, stone circles and other megalithic monuments provided a permanent backdrop to the everyday environment within which the ordinary country people of Ireland lived and toiled, perhaps the legacy represented by these monuments blended in *too* well, for among the intellectuals who shaped Ireland's growth to modern nationhood this aspect of their heritage – despite its obvious longevity – was surprisingly ignored. To the newly emergent and enthusiastic breed of romantics, literary figures and idealists another part of this island's past seemed much more vibrant and potent – its Celtic legacy.

And one can understand why this should be so, for Ireland's Celtic legacy is enduring and spectacular, its richness nowhere better exemplified than in its primary gift to the Irish people – a beautiful and poetic language. However, the intense pride occasioned by this Celtic legacy, so opportunely harnessed to the new mood of national self-assertiveness, unfortunately pushed into the background the more ancient heritage which had preceded it – an inheritance dating back to those who had established the very basis of the Irish personality, long before a Celt had ever set foot upon these shores.

So all-pervasive has been the 'Celtic legacy' that most Irish men and women are still content to assume that they have been part of a 'pure' Celtic race from time immemorial. For others, however, doubts frequently surface, especially when they endeavour to probe deeper into the origins of the people of this island. Connemara author Bob Quinn described the frustration which constantly confronted him during his own search:

> Everything unusual or distinctive about Ireland seemed to be, consciously or unconsciously, lumped into the vague category 'Celtic'. The 'Celts' were becoming, for me, a historical cul-de-sac beyond which investigation was almost pointless.[16]

Others found that their studies threw up conclusions which were at variance with commonly-held notions, as when folklorist Kevin Danaher sought to explore the origins of the Irish four-season calendar. He concluded that

> the four-season calendar of modern Irish tradition is of very high antiquity, even of late neolithic or megalithic origin, and that its beginnings predate the early Celts in Ireland by at least as great a depth of time as that which separates those early Celts from us. . . . One lesson which we might learn from this is that we cannot necessarily assume that because something is early Irish it is therefore Celtic. There is at least an even chance that it may be pre-Celtic. . . . We might even go further, and ask if we are not straining the bounds of scientific credibility by claiming that the Irish are a Celtic people?[16]

Other scholars came to similar conclusions.

> It is difficult to believe that the immense store of lore and custom associated with festivals such as Lughnasa, occurring at the beginning of autumn, or 'harvest', whose present-day survivals, including the ever popular pilgrimage to the rocky summit of Croag Patrick, have been brilliantly documented and interpreted by Maire MacNeill, do not contain a large pre-Celtic element, particularly where they concern high hilltops and rivers and lakes. Wakes for the

dead, fairy-lore and animal-lore also seem to have ancient roots.[10]

However, while at one time any suggestion that the Irish were not a pure Celtic race might have stirred up much controversy, even resentment, such a situation no longer pertains today. Increasingly, archaeologists and historians acknowledge that the Celts, notwithstanding their enduring legacy, were undoubtedly never more than a small minority within the Irish population. As Peter Woodman made clear:

> The gene pool of the Irish was probably set by the end of the Stone Age when there were very substantial numbers of people present and the landscape had already been frequently altered. The Irish are essentially Pre-Indo-European, they are not physically Celtic. No invasion since could have been sufficiently large to alter that fact completely.[17]

Those engaged in the study of linguistics came to a similar conclusion.*

> As to the Celtic invasions and subsequent occupation of the British Isles little is known. It is likely that they did not involve large numbers of Indo-European-speaking people, a view which has led a number of scholars, including myself, to believe that in the British Isles Indo-European language as imposed by small bands of Celtic invaders from the Continent must

---

* This has been confirmed by modern DNA studies. The authors of an article in *The Sunday Times* 22.03.98, 'Britons stand united on the DNA map', report that the first genetic survey of the British Isles, carried out by Oxford University, reveals that the people of the British Isles 'are united by common DNA that dates back at least 10,000 years to the last Ice Age'. Even the combined invasions of the Celts, Romans, Anglo-Saxons, Vikings and Normans made only 'minimal impact' upon the 'much more powerful inheritance' of the ancient inhabitants.'

have been influenced strongly by the speaking habits of a predominantly non-Celtic population.[18]

It is rewarding to look at the Gaelic language in the light of the abundant evidence for the survival of population from pre-Celtic times – in the light of the Irish heritage. As Professor David Greene has declared with patriotic pride: 'Irish is a language made in Ireland: it is neither Indo-European nor Celtic, Pictish or Hamitic, but simply the linguistic expression of the Irish people.'[10]

Hence today, even though a few scholars remain guarded in their opinions – one cautiously stating that 'it is very likely that there may have been a strong pre-Celtic element in the population'[19] – a growing number within academia now accept that the Celts only constituted a minority in Ireland, albeit a powerful one, although at the same time accepting that popular perception still continues to deem otherwise:

The idea of a mass Celticisation of Ireland during the last half of the last millennium BC is still widely believed, with the implication that the population that had been building up over several thousand years . . . suddenly metamorphosed into a Celtic race.[20]

21

The Cruthin

As we now know that the Celts only comprised a minority within the population, an intriguing question arises: who then made up the bulk of the Irish people when they become known to us at the dawn of our written history? Were they direct descendants of the Mesolithic, Neolithic and Bronze Age populations? Were they other non-Celtic peoples who came to Ireland just prior to the arrival of the Celts? Were they a mixture of these? There is no definite answer as such to these questions, only theories and probabilities.

What we *can* say, however, is that archaeologists have found no evidence of any sizeable intrusion into Ireland subsequent to the Neolithic period, indicating that at the time the Celts arrived the bulk of the Irish population basically reflected the more ancient population groups. Such a continuity with the past was assumed by Richard Warner when he assessed cultural intrusions into Ireland in the Early Iron Age:

> Throughout our period the mass of the Irish people remained racially unchanged. Whatever they were at the end of the Bronze Age they were still, with a small but important addition (partly at least from the Celtic world), when they entered the early medieval period.[20]

The Greek geographer and voyager Pytheas, some time between 330 and 300 BC, provided us with the earliest reference to the British Isles, calling them the 'Isles of the Pretani' (*Pretanikai nesoi*), thereby making these Pretani the most ancient inhabitants of Great Britain (Albion) and Ireland (Little Britain) to whom a definite name can be given. In classical writings a variety of forms of the name is found, including the later *Britanni*, or 'British'. In Gaelic 'Pretani' would become 'Cruithni', the name of one of the main population groups mentioned by the ancient Irish writers, and also the name used by these same writers when referring to the Picts of Scotland, those northern British who had never been conquered by Rome. As historian Francis Byrne pointed out:

> The earlier, non-Indo-European, population, of course, survived under the Celtic overlordship. One group in particular, known to the P-Celts as *Pritani* and to the Irish as *Cruithni*, survived into historical times as the Picts or 'painted people' of Scotland. The Cruithni were numerous in Ulster too, and the Loíges of Leinster and possibly the Ciarraige of Connacht and north Kerry belonged to the same people.[21]

Two important questions arise here: firstly, just how close was this suggested relationship between the 'Irish Cruthin' and the 'Scottish Picts'; and secondly, how prominent were the Cruthin within Ireland itself?

When medieval Irish writers refer to the Cruthin, the Ireland/ Scotland connection is frequently asserted. One writer stated that 'thirty kings of the Cruthin ruled Ireland and Scotland from Ollam to Fiachna mac Baetáin' and that 'seven kings of the Cruthin of Scotland ruled Ireland in Tara' (*secht rig do Chruithnibh Alban rofhallnastair Erind i Temair*). Others refer to Scotland as the 'land of the Cruthin', while in a poem written in the eleventh or twelfth century the author tells us that the *Cruthnig* made up a section of the population of Scotland. The Annals of Tigernach, The Pictish Chronicle, St Berchan, the Albanic Duan, the Book of Deer and John of Fordun plainly show that the name Cruthin was applied to the inhabitants of both Scotland and Ireland.

The persistence of the ancient writers in this matter was so strong that even when the early genealogists eventually fabricated a 'Gaelic' pedigree for the Cruthin, the latter's more ancient origin legends still survived, as T F O'Rahilly noted:

> The combined influence of Bede, Mael Mura, and the [genealogists] caused *Cruithni* to lose favour as the name of a section of the Irish population. This disuse of *Cruithni* as a name is doubtless connected with the rise of a new genealogical doctrine which turned the Irish Cruthin into Goidels and thus disassociated them from the Cruthin of Scotland. Nevertheless the fact that there were Cruthin in Ireland as well as in Scotland was, as might be expected, long remembered; and so it is not surprising to find writers occasionally suggesting, in defiance of Mael Mura, that the Cruthin of both countries formed one people in remote times.[22]

However, such ancient literary references to an Irish/Scottish connection are not considered as reliable 'evidence' by some scholars. As Charles Doherty stated: 'If the Cruthin were ever the same people as the Picts of Scotland it was in the very remote past, because in the historical period there is no connection between the two people.'[19] Doherty's conclusion is partly based on the fact that 'there is no archaeological evidence to suggest a Pictish connection.' Yet 'archaeological evidence' is not always available to confirm historically attested events, as was admitted by Mallory and McNeill with regard to a later period in our history:

> History records how towards the end of the 5th century AD Ulstermen began conquering and colonizing southwestern Scotland to form the kingdom of Dál Riata which spanned the northern region of the Irish

Sea ... despite the fact that we believe we know
when all this took place, there is really not a shred of
archaeological evidence to prove that it did happen.[23]

And just as events *subsequent* to the 5th century reveal an
ongoing connection between Ulster and Scotland, there is
nothing to suggest that such a connection was not a reality *prior*
to that period as well. And we do not have to rely merely upon
the insistence of the ancient Irish writers of a possible kinship
link. As far back as the Stone Age there is archaeological
evidence of population contact. Identical burial monuments
from that period have been excavated in both the north of
Ireland and south-west Scotland, leading Séan O Ríordáin to
comment: 'The tombs and the finds from them form a continuous
province joined rather than divided by the narrow waters of the
North Channel.'[24] Certainly, the geographical proximity of
Ulster to Scotland would easily facilitate the same people
establishing themselves on both sides of the North Channel, it
being only thirteen miles wide at its narrowest point.

Hence, even if the archaeological and historical evidence
may not allow us at present to establish the exact extent of any
possible kinship between the pre-Celtic peoples of Scotland
and Ulster, at the same time there is nothing which necessarily
contradicts the assertion of the ancient writers that the Cruthin
of both areas formed one people in remote times. Indeed, some
scholars do afford it credibility; in the latest edition of *The
Oxford Illustrated History of Ireland*, Donnchadh Ó Corráin
writes:

What is interesting, too, is the mixed racial and
linguistic background of the rulers of Ireland – Britain
and Ireland share languages, dominant aristocracies,
and whole local populations such as the Cruithin of
Ireland and Scotland (where they are known to Latin
writers as Picti).[25]

25

Furthermore, many academics now accept that the relationship between the peoples on either side of the North Channel was a close one. Liam de Paor concluded:

> The gene pool of the Irish . . . is probably very closely related to the gene pools of highland Britain. . . Within that fringe area, relationships, both cultural and genetic, almost certainly go back to a much more distant time than that uncertain period when Celtic languages and customs came to dominate both Great Britain and Ireland. Therefore, so far as the physical make-up of the Irish goes . . . they share these origins with their fellows in the neighbouring parts – the north and west – of the next-door island of Great Britain.[26]

A similar problem of verification arises with regard to the second question: how widespread were the Cruthin in Ireland? One ancient account of the 'Milesian' invasion (the origin legend of the Gaels) – known as 'Laud 610' – tells us

> how 'the second Míl Espáne', as it calls the leader of the Goidelic invaders of the Eastern Midlands, found the Cruithnig . . . dominant (i.e. in the northern half of Ireland), and how the invaders fought many battles with them. Until the time of Conn Cétchathach, we are told, every alternate king of Ireland was of the Cruithnig.[22]

One nineteenth century writer undoubtedly took some of the medieval writers too much at face value when he remarked: 'No fact in the pagan history of Ireland is more certain than that the whole country was originally held by the Irish Picts.'[27] Another writer was just as assertive:

> Here it is needful to state that the Picts, or Cruithne, of Clanna Rury, once possessed, according to popular

belief, the whole of Ulster. It is highly probable that at one time they possessed, not only Ulster, but the greater part of Ireland.[28]

However, these days we must be far more circumspect, and until evidence emerges which could allow us to state otherwise all we can postulate is that the Cruthin were to be found in those areas of Ireland identified by historians from their study of the ancient texts (as in map below, by F J Byrne[21]). And the main focus of their power and influence was the kingdom of the Dál nAraidi, later to become known as Dalaradia.

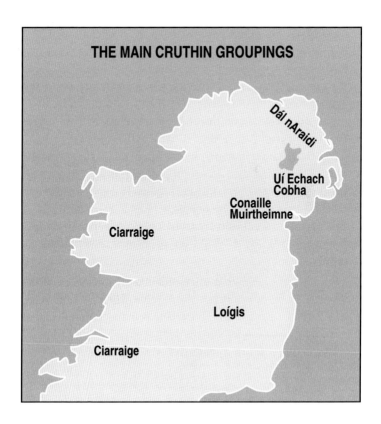

THE MAIN CRUTHIN GROUPINGS

Dál nAraidi

Uí Echach
Cobha
Conaille
Muirtheimne
Ciarraige

Loígis

Ciarraige

First Glimpses

When Irish history first begins to be written down, around the fifth century AD, we find a complex web of kingdoms struggling for either supremacy or survival. According to the ancient writers and genealogists there existed different ethnic groupings – such as the Érainn, Cruthin, and Lagin – each of which had distinct origin legends and ancestral traditions, so persistent that even as these groups became assimilated into an increasingly homogeneous Irish society, they nevertheless retained memories of their separate identities well into the early middle ages.

The Érainn (the *Iverni* recorded by Ptolemy on his map in the second century), according to their own traditions, came to Ireland from Great Britain, where they had already gained power. The Érainn were in origin Belgae and took their name from the river Iernos, probably the modern Roughty in Munster. The later Lagin were Domnonians.

Irish society was basically tribal, with each tribe – *tuath* – being ruled over by a king. In popular imagery medieval 'kings' were individuals whose sovereignty extended over vast realms, and the presumed governance of the 'High-Kings of Ireland' was no exception. The reality, however, was quite different, as Francis Byrne explained:

> In fact, there were probably no less than 150 kings in the country at any given date between the fifth and twelfth centuries. . . . Even the most powerful of high-kings was basically ruler of a single *tuath*, and

exercised no direct authority outside it. In later ages this multiplication of monarchies caused some embarrassment to patriotic Irishmen who had been brought up to believe in the glories of the high-kingship of Ireland centred in Tara. ... The title *ard-rí*, 'high-king', is not very old, nor is it found in the legal texts. It has no precise significance, and does not necessarily imply sovereignty of Ireland.[5]

One remarkable – and still existent – antiquity, which has been dated to the centuries just prior to the written period, is the remnant of a long earthwork 'wall' which stretches, in a broken series of sections, across the 'neck' of Ireland, from Bundoran on the west to South Armagh on the east. What was the purpose of this wall, traditionally known as the 'Black Pig's Dyke'? Was it merely a 'hindrance to cattle-stealing', as some have insisted, or did its existence hint at some territorial, even political, significance? Aiden Walsh investigated one section of the earthwork in County Monaghan:

Firstly, the Black Pig's Dyke was not simply a two-line defence (double-bank and double-ditch); it was a three-line defence. The third line was composed of a timber palisade which paralleled the earthwork itself. Secondly, it is clear from [its] scale and nature that we are dealing with a defensive structure. The earthwork also faces south and is set on southern facing slopes to defend those on its northern side. Thirdly, it appears to have been deliberately and quite fully destroyed, presumably during wartime. The short excavation carried out in County Monaghan has told us that this stretch of the monument . . . was built in the last few centuries BC. Perhaps we are dealing here with . . . a war extending across the land starting at the boundaries of a kingdom and culminating with the destruction of its capital.[29]

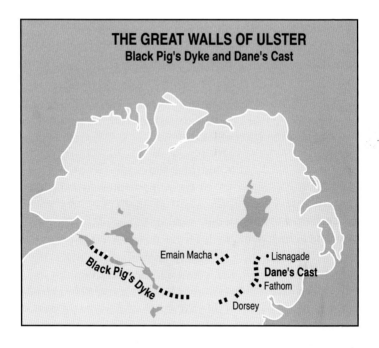

THE GREAT WALLS OF ULSTER
Black Pig's Dyke and Dane's Cast

Black Pig's Dyke

Emain Macha

Dorsey

Lisnagade

Dane's Cast

Fathom

What sort of events could have been occurring in the North of Ireland during the last few centuries BC or the first few centuries AD? Some scholars have suggested that tantalising glimpses into the politics of that period are possibly enshrined in the group of tales known as The Ulster Cycle, which, although not written down until centuries later, are felt to relate to the first few centuries of the Christian era. The centrepiece of the tales, the *Táin Bó Cuailnge* (to be discussed later), depicts a North dominated by a warrior caste, the Ulaid, and engaged in constant warfare with the armies of the 'men of Ireland'.

Whether these tales reflect genuine memories of actual warfare is impossible to ascertain. Certainly Francis Byrne feels that this literature 'cannot be properly understood except as historical documentation'.[5] But most scholars, Byrne included, would hesitate to draw more than tentative associations; the historical and archaeological evidence is presently insufficient to allow us to do otherwise.

One thing is certain, however: the 'ancient Ulster' depicted so vividly in the sagas – and which dominated the entire North of Ireland – was only a memory in the eighth century when the sagas were committed to writing, for by that time the Ulstermen – particularly the Cruthin and the Ulaid – had been pushed east of the River Bann and were struggling to retain their autonomy. This dramatic change in their fortunes had been occasioned by one section of the population who had by then become totally dominant in Irish politics – the Goidels, or Gaels.

The Gaels, in some of their origin legends, trace their ancestry back to Tuathal Techtmar, whose mother was said to be British. The earliest account of his conquest of Ireland from the *aithechthuatha*, the non-Gaelic vassal tribes, is found in a poem by Mael Mura of Othain (AD 885). Mael Mura dates the invasion to about 135 AD, though other sources provide alternative dates. But all accounts agree on the details of his invasion: he arrived with an army of foreigners on the east coast of Ireland, conquering the tribes there and carving out a 'midland' Gaelic colony by force of arms.

From the Midland Gaels a few centuries later came a person who bridges the link between mythical and real history – Niall Noígiallach ('Niall of the Nine Hostages'). Niall, who also had a British mother, reigned in Tara during the first quarter of the fifth century. It was Niall who founded that great Gaelic dynasty, the Uí Néill ('descendants of Niall'), from whom the later O'Neills would spring.

One of those who gives credence to Tuathal Techtmar as being an actual historical personage is Richard Warner, who

31

also advances the theory, which he bases on existing archeological evidence, that Techtmar's arrival (with a retinue, Warner suggests, of 'Romanised Irishmen and Roman-Gaulish and Romano-British adventurers') constitutes strong circumstantial support for a Roman incursion into Ireland, something hitherto considered unacceptable to most Irish historians. Warner feels such a scenario would at the very least help clear up a number of problems.

> It has always been difficult to understand why the Goidels, and particularly the dynasties descended from Niall, seemed to appear from nowhere to gain political dominance in a couple of centuries. If we equate their rise to the fact that they came from Britain with all the benefits of Roman training, weapons and organisation we are less surprised.[30]

My own opinion is that the earliest 'Celtic' incursions were of the Belgic Érainn, Menapii, and Brigantes, followed by the Domnonian Lagin, and that Tuathal Techtmar was a later Roman soldier or auxiliary originally from Spain (Míl Espáne).

Whatever the reasons for their rise to prominence, and wherever they came from, or when, the establishment of Gaelic hegemony represented a major new approach to political organisation in Ireland. This was epitomised most dramatically by undoubtedly the most prominent section among the Gaels, the Uí Néill, and the dynastic manner in which they parcelled out their conquests was a radical departure from the purely tribal society which had preceded them.

To invest these conquests with the authority of legitimacy, the Uí Néill established themselves as High-Kings of Ireland, centred around their base in Tara, and in later centuries their literary élite would attempt to portray this lineage as having stretched back into the remote past. However, such a claim has since been discounted, as Byrne remarked:

It is now evident that Niall and his descendents for many centuries can in no real sense be described as high-kings of all Ireland. The claims made for them in the late seventh century by Adomnán and Muirchú . . . must be discounted as partisan: few other contemporary documents show special deference being afforded to the Uí Néill outside their own sphere of influence, and the laws do not even envisage the office of high-king of Ireland.[5]

The Struggle for Ulster

Having subdued the midland area around Meath, Niall and his sons turned their attention northwards – to the ancient territory of Ulster. It is difficult to believe that the political situation within Ulster at that time possessed anything like the cohesiveness and centralisation implicit in the sagas. The reality was undoubtedly more complex, and one which reflected the tensions existing between the different groupings within the northern population. However, it does seem that the geographical extent of Ulster as depicted in the sagas was reasonably accurate, covering as it did the entire north of the island and stretching as far south as the River Boyne.

It has been suggested that the Ulaid, from whom Ulster gets it name, were possibly La Téne Celts from Britain, holding sway over the North from Emain Macha near Armagh. Byrne points out that the 'general truth of the Ulster traditions is to some extent corroborated by archaeology, since the rather scanty La Téne remains in Ireland tend to be concentrated in the north'.[5] However, there is no evidence to suggest a major intrusion by these Celts, and it is probable that the Ulaid, like their Uí Néill opponents, were a warrior caste endeavouring to impose their overlordship upon indigenous tribes. Among these indigenous tribes the most prominent were the Cruthin, still powerful enough to share the over-kingship of Ulster with the Ulaid, even at times to assert that they, and not the Ulaid, were the 'true Ulstermen'.

Ancient tradition has it that some time before the reign of Niall Noígiallach, an attack on Ulster had already been initiated by three brothers, the 'Three Collas', relatives of the then king of Tara, Muiredach Tírech, although some scholars doubt this tradition and feel that the actual invasion was the work of Niall and his sons. Standish Hayes O'Grady has given the following rendition of that tradition:

> The Collas asked: 'what country dost thou of thy power the most readily assign us, that we make swordland of it? (for warriors better than the Collas there were none). Muiredach said: 'attack Ulster; they are not kindly disposed to us.' But yonder was a warrior force too great for the Collas; so they went to the men of Connacht, and became their protégés, and they received them. Subsequently Connacht came with them, seven battalions strong all told, and they were at the cairn of *Achadh lethderg* in Farney, in Ulster. From that cairn they deliver seven battles against Ulster, one daily to a week's end: being six fought by Connacht and one by the Collas. Every single day Ulster was routed; the Collas' battle was on the last day; recreant failure in fighting was none there; the battle was maintained for a summer's day and night, till blood reached shields; hard by the cairn is *coll na nothar* 'Hazel of the Wounded'. [In this last battle] Ulster gave way at break of the second day; the slaughter lasted as far as Glenree. A week then the others spent harrying Ulster, and they made swordland of the country.[31]

In the far west of Ulster the Uí Néill conquest was the most complete. There, three of Niall's sons, Connall, Eogan (Owen) and Enda, established their own kingdoms. The territory of Connall, now Donegal, became known as Tir-Connall (the land of Connall), and from Connall were descended the O'Donnells.

The territory of Owen was Inishowen (the island of Owen). The Clan Owen later expanded into Tir Owen, which is now Tyrone. From Owen descended the Northern O'Neills, the McLoughlins, O'Kanes, O'Hagans, O'Mullans, Devlins and other Gaelic planters. Niall's remaining sons stayed in control of the Midlands.

The capital of Ulster at Emain Macha seems to have either fallen to the Uí Néill, or been abandoned by the Ulstermen, around the year 450.

In 563 the Northern Uí Néill confronted the Cruthin at the great battle of Móin Dairi Lothair (Moneymore). Seven kings of the Cruthin were killed and the way was open for the Northern Uí Néill victors to expand into what is now County Londonderry. In the *Annals of Ulster* the compiler, when recording the battle, also depicted it in verse:

> Sharp weapons stretch, men stretch
> In the great bog of Daire-lothair –
> The cause of a contention for right –
> Seven Cruithnian Kings, including Aedh Brecc.
> The Battle of all the Cruithni is fought,
> [And] they burn Eilne.
> The battle of Gahair-Lifè is fought,
> And the battle of Cul-dreimne.

Two years later the Cruthin over-king of Ulster, Aed Dub mac Suibni, slew the Northern Uí Néill king, Diarmait mac Cerbaill. A battle is also recorded between the Cruthin and the Uí Néill near Coleraine in 579.

In that part of Ulster lying to the south-west of Lough Neagh, a number of vassal tribes, known to us by the collective name of the Airgialla (the name also given to their territory), either took the opportunity to declare their autonomy or managed to co-exist precariously between the Uí Néill and the retreating Ulstermen.

The boundary between Airgialla and the now-reduced territory of Ulster was given permanence by the construction of another massive earthwork wall similar to the Black Pig's Dyke, running along the vale of the Newry River. It extended from Lisnagade one mile north-east of Scarva in County Down, to near Meigh, not far from Killeavy and Slieve Gullion in County Armagh. Parts of this earthwork, much later erroneously named 'Dane's Cast', can still be seen today.

One investigation of the 'Cast' was undertaken in 1815 by John Bell, a landscape painter turned surveyor. The enthusiasm he brought to his task is evident from this account:

> There is a tradition in the Reilly family that [Bell] arrived at Scarvagh House . . . and started early in the day to examine the 'Cast', promising to be back at seven o'clock for dinner; but he did not appear till the small hours of the next morning, having become so enthusiastic in his investigations as to find himself at sunset nearer Newry than Scarvagh.[32]

In its construction the 'Cast' consists of a wide fosse or trench with a rampart on either side. The numerous raths and duns on the eastern side, coupled with the vast quantity of ancient arms found in the vicinity, would seem to indicate that the area was densely populated by a strong military force. The chief fortifications were at Lisnagade, Fathom, Crown Mound, Terney and Listullyard. Fathom was an important link in this chain of fortifications, as it commanded approaches through Moyry Pass – the 'gap of the North'. This defence system was to remain politically effective for the next two hundred years.

The Kingdom of Dalaradia

It was the Cruthin who formed the bulk of the population within the now much-reduced Ulster. There is evidence of the existence of from seven to nine petty kingdoms of the Cruthin, formed into a loose confederation. North-west of the Lower Bann dwelled the Cruthin of Arda Eolairg and the Li. In present-day County Down, another branch of the Cruthin, the Uí Echach Cobha, inhabited the present baronies of Upper and Lower Iveagh and Kinelarty. However, the main dynasty among the Cruthin was the Dál nAraidi, and the area they controlled became known in English as 'Dalaradia' (not to be confused with Dalriada further to the north-east). The northern Dál nAraidi extended from Lough Neagh northwards to the sea between the mouths of the rivers Bush and Bann, and included Coleraine and its environs. They also inhabited the area east of the Bann to the sea at Larne, which bore the name Latharna.

Despite the Cruthin forming the bulk of the population in this reduced Ulster, it was their main rivals the Ulaid – particularly the most dominant dynasty within the Ulaid, the Dál Fiatach (ruling over the maritime areas between Dundrum Bay and Belfast Lough, with the centre of their power established at Downpatrick) – who dominated the over-kingship of Ulster, though not without opposition, as Francis Byrne noted:

> The Cruthin on occasion usurped the over-kingship of Ulaid: more often than not they bore the brunt of the wars against the Uí Néill. They became bold enough

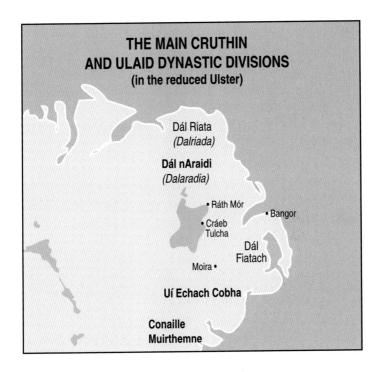

THE MAIN CRUTHIN
AND ULAID DYNASTIC DIVISIONS
(in the reduced Ulster)

Dál Riata
(Dalriada)

Dál nAraidi
(Dalaradia)

• Ráth Mór
• Bangor
• Cráeb
Tulcha
Dál
Fiatach
Moira •

Uí Echach Cobha

Conaille
Muirthemne

to claim that they, and not the Dál Fiatach, were the fír-Ulaid, the 'true Ulstermen'.[5]

Indeed, legend has it that Tuathal Techtmar met his death in battle in the heartland of Dál nAraidi territory, and in 565 the Northern Uí Néill king, Diarmait mac Cerbaill, met his death close to the royal seat of the Dál nAraidi, at Ráth Mór, a few miles east of Antrim town. Not that the Uí Néill were the only foes: Belfast received its first mention in history, in 667, for being the location of a battle between the Cruthin and the Ulaid at the 'Fearsat', the sandbank or ford of the Lagan river.

The inauguration stone of the kings of Ulster, and probably of the kings of Dalaradia, was reputedly located at the Hill of

39

Crew, at Glenavy near Lough Neagh, some ten miles south of the Royal residence of Ráth Mór Moy Linny. According to R G Berry:

> . . . it was the highest hill in Ulster, 629 feet high, and situated two miles to the south east of Glenavy, where it surveys the surrounding countryside. Called *Craobh Tulcha* [Cráeb Tulcha] in ancient times (now Crew Hill), this has been translated at 'the tree of the hill' and under this tree, which in pagan times was regarded as sacred, stood the inauguration stone of the Kings of Ulster.'[33]

Although Uí Néill territorial gains had resulted in ancient Ulster being greatly reduced in size, over the next few centuries the Ulaid and Cruthin leaders proved themselves quite capable of halting any further territorial encroachments, and undoubtedly they even retained hopes of regaining their lost territory. As Byrne commented:

> It seems that the collapse of the Ulaid was not total nor regarded as irreversible. They . . . and their Cruthin associates certainly were to remain for many generations a much more powerful force than later historians of the Uí Néill high-kingship cared to remember.[5]

The Power of the Word

While the martially-inclined were deciding contentious issues on the field of battle, others in Ulster were engaged in more peaceful and creative activities. None more so than the *filid*, who were held in high regard in Irish society, as Eleanor Hull explained:

> The laws, the genealogies of the clans, the history of the tribes, were all composed and recited in verse. Consequently, the most important persons in the land, next to the chiefs, were the Filés. It was their business to act as law-givers, arbitrators, genealogists, and historians, besides being the story-tellers and poets of the tribes. They were treated with the greatest respect, and were constantly in attendance on the chief, taking part in his councils. It was not simply in order to remember the laws and annals more easily, before writing was invented, that they were recited in verse, as some people seem to think; it was also to add dignity to them.[34]

The *Ollam*, or chief *filí*, was obliged to be able to recite, on any particular occasion, any of the three hundred and fifty stories which it was his duty to have memorised. High standards were set for the *Ollam*; according to one text he was to be possessed of 'purity of learning, purity of mouth (that is, he was not to satirise unjustly), purity of hand (from blood-letting), purity of marriage, and purity (or honesty) from theft and robbery.' The ancient texts also inform us, however, that not all the *filid* met such high expectations. Nevertheless, the role they played was of great significance, and tells us much about Irish society.

> In some ways it could be argued that the *filid* wielded more power than did the kings. They moulded public opinion, which is the ultimate arbiter of acceptable forms of polity and policy. . . . There can be little doubt that the influence which they exerted so effectively for over a thousand years was rooted in ancient belief in the power of the word.[5]

Into Irish society with this deep respect for the 'word' was to intrude, in the fifth century, an equally vibrant force – Christianity. To the Irish, credit for the introduction of Christianity belongs to St Patrick, although scholars accept that there were Christians in Ireland before his coming. The only first-hand accounts of Patrick actually come from two works which he reputedly wrote himself: the *Confession* and the *Epistle to Coroticus*. According to legend Patrick was first brought to Ireland as a slave from Romanised Britain and sold to a Cruthin chieftain called Milchu, a petty king who ruled over part of Dalaradia near Mount Slemish, in present-day County Antrim. (A rival claim, however, locates Patrick's place of captivity in County Mayo.)

After six years of servitude Patrick managed to escape from Ireland, perhaps going to Gaul, and two years later was finally reunited with his parents in Britain. Patrick then had a vision in which an angel brought him letters from Ireland, one of which contained the appeal: 'We beg you, Holy youth, to come and walk amongst us once again.' To Patrick, the letters 'completely broke my heart and I could read no more and woke up.' He decided to return, and although we do not know exactly where he received his ecclesiastical training, one seventh-century biography makes him a disciple of St Germanus of Auxerre in Gaul. It would appear that it was Germanus who sent Patrick to Celestine, the Bishop of Rome, to receive authority for a mission to Ireland.

Tradition has it that in 432 Patrick eventually made his way back to Ireland, landing in County Down in the territory of Dichu (of the Ulaid) who became his first convert. Dichu's barn (sabhall or Saul) near Downpatrick was the first of his churches.

Among Patrick's first converts were Bronagh, daughter of Milchu, and her son Mochaoi (Mahee). St Mochaoi was to found the great monastery of Nendrum on Mahee Island in Loch Cuan (Strangford Lough), and is associated with the saint in the legends which grew around Patrick's name. These legends firmly place Down as the cradle of Christianity in Ireland. At Nendrum were first educated Colman, who was of the Cruthin, and Finnian, who was of the Ulaid. Colman was to found the famous See of Dromore in Iveagh, while Finnian was to found the great school of Movilla (Newtownards) in Down.

Patrick himself is said to have founded Armagh around 444, and the selection of a site so close to Emain Macha would strongly suggest that the Ulster capital was still the most powerful over-kingdom in Ireland at that time. And while the Irish church was not to reach its apogee until after Patrick's death, we should not underestimate the debt owed to this great 'Apostle of Ireland', whose importance, rather than diminishing under modern critical analysis, seems to be growing in stature, as Charles Doherty noted:

> Our approach to Patrick, the historical human being, must be through his own writings which are profoundly spiritual statements. The qualities of this great saint shine through them. Patrick's humility – that what he does and what he has achieved are not as a result of

> his will but that of God acting through him – permeates his writings. Until recently scholars have taken Patrick's claim of lack of learning at face value and declared him to be a man of one book – the Bible. Now [some] scholars . . . argue that his reading of the Fathers was extensive and they have examined his theology and reassessed his intellectual stature.[35]

Whereas in the modern era the spread of Christianity around the world was often marked by an arrogant disregard for other people's cultures and belief systems – something now acknowledged and regretted by many in the Church – in Ireland, although paganism put up strong resistance to the new faith, the Church was wise enough to adapt itself to many ancient Irish beliefs and customs, and where possible to 'Christianise' them. It could not have been otherwise, for the existing culture was too deep-rooted within the ordinary people to have been easily eradicated. And ancient traditions would have been fiercely defended by the *filid*. In fact, it was not in the destruction of paganism and ancient Irish ways which saw the Church rise triumphant, but in the cross-fertilisation which resulted.

> The Christian clergy had no monopoly of learning . . . Tribal law and custom was no vague body of lore dependent on the memory of the oldest men. It was jealously preserved in druidical schools by a professional class who quickly profited by the new learning of the monasteries to become literate in their own language and commit the tradition to writing. . . . Irish monasticism cultivated learning and so ensured respect in a society where scholarship was held in high regard.[5]

The fusion which ensued, as ancient beliefs and traditions merged with the new Christian faith, was to produce a vibrant cultural renaissance.

The Elder Faiths are part of the Irish heritage. It was cultural diversity and cross fertilisation between pagan and Christian that brought into being what will always count as Ireland's greatest cultural achievements in the Golden Age of the seventh and eight centuries: the Books of Durrow and Kells, the Ardagh Chalice, the great Celtic monasteries and countless works of art and architecture.[10]

As we shall shortly see, this explosion of creativity was to enrich not only Ireland, but the wider world beyond.

St Comgall and Bangor

One of the most important figures in the history of the early Church was Comgall, undoubtedly the most famous Cruthin of all. He was born, it is said, in 512 at Magheramorne, County Antrim, in Dalaradia. Comgall was educated under St Fintan at Clonenagh, and is also said to have studied under Finnian at Clonard and Mobhi Clairenach at Glasnevin. Following his ordination, Comgall was imbued with a great missionary zeal and his greatest achievement was the founding of a monastic settlement at Bangor on the coast of County Down. To distinguish it from the other Bangors in the British Isles it became known as Bangor Mór, 'Bangor the Great'.

> Such was his reputation for piety and learning that multitudes flocked to his school from the most distant parts; it is well established that not less than 3,000 students and teachers were under his care at one time, including many of the most honourable in the land. The evangelistic zeal of Comgall was pre-eminent – down to the landing-place at the reef of rocks he led many a band of his disciples who were to embark on their frail coracles to spread the Gospel in European countries.[36]

Life at Bangor was severe. The food was sparse and even milk was considered an indulgence. Only one meal per day was allowed and that not until evening. Confession was held in public before the whole community and severe acts of penance were observed. There was silence during meals and at other times conversation was restricted to the minimum.

The strength of the community lay in its form of worship. The choral services were based on the antiphonal singing from Gaul, introduced into the West by Ambrose of Milan in the fourth century. Bangor became famous for this type of choral psalmody and it spread from there throughout Europe once more. The glory of Bangor was the celebration of a perfected and refined *Laus Perennis*, and because of the great number of students and monks attached to Bangor and its outlying daughter churches, it was possible to have a continuous chorus of the Divine Praise sung by large choirs divided into groups.

One of the most important religious works produced at Bangor was the *Bangor Antiphonary*, now housed in Italy, though not always accessible to the passing visitor – even one who would later become Primate of Ireland:

> Twenty years ago I paid my first visit to Bobbio in northern Italy where the manuscript of the Antiphonary of Bangor was lovingly preserved for many centuries. I then proceeded to Milan in order to see the manuscript itself in its present home in the Ambrosian Library. Imagine my frustration when I discovered that although the Library had reopened after the summer vacation, the manuscript room would not reopen for visitors until the following week. As my return ticket did not allow me to stay over, I pleaded with the Library authorities and pulled out all the stops: . . . came all the way from near Bangor . . . would only take a minute . . . was a professor of history . . . but all to no avail. Every time a member of the staff passed in or out of the room I could see that there were manuscripts on show in the glass cases within . . . But I did not see the manuscript of the Antiphonary for another three years.[37]

The creed found in the *Bangor Antiphonary* differs in wording from all known others and is in substance the original Creed of Nicaea. For this reason alone it may be considered one of the most precious relics of Western civilisation. In the *Antiphonary*, there is a celebration of Bangor's contribution to church history.

> The Holy, valiant deeds
> Of sacred Fathers,
> Based on the matchless
> Church of Bangor;
> The noble deeds of abbots,
> Their number, times and names,
> Of never-ending lustre,
> Hear, brothers; great their deserts,
> > Whom the Lord hath gathered
> > To the mansions of his heavenly kingdom,
> Christ loved Comgall,
> Well, too, did he the Lord.

Descriptions of what such monastic settlements looked like have been preserved for us in ancient manuscripts.

> From Adomnán's Life of Colum Cille, written in Iona in the seventh century, when some of those who had entered the monastery under the founder were still alive, we can reconstruct the authentic picture in great detail. Instead of a communal residence, the monks lived in individual cells constructed of wood or wattles, the abbot's cell slightly apart from the rest. Besides the cells of the monks the monastic enclosure included within it the *church*, usually built of oak, with a stone altar, sacred vessels, relics and handbells for summoning the congregation; the *refectory* with its long table, and adjoining it the *kitchen* containing an open fire, cooking utensils, and a large cauldron of drinking water; the *library* and *scriptorium* with manuscripts suspended in satchels by leather straps from the walls and an ample supply of writing materials

– waxed tablets, parchment, quills and stylos, ink-horns and the rest. A workshop and forge were situated nearby, while outside the rampart came the cultivated lands and pastures belonging to the monastery, furnished with farm buildings and in addition a mill and limekiln.[38]

Another of the great religious figures of Ireland was Columba (Colum-Cille), a prince of the Northern Uí Néill; his father, it is claimed, was the great-grandson of Niall of the Nine Hostages. Columba studied under St Finnian at Movilla, where he was ordained deacon. According to the *Annals of Ulster*, Columba founded Derry in 545. He became a close friend of Comgall's, even though the political and ethnic rivalries between their respective kinsmen must at times have sorely tested that friendship.

Columba's biographer, Adamnan, the ninth abbot of Iona from 679-704, describes an encounter between the two great churchmen which not only highlights the communal conflicts of the period, but conveys with some pathos the sadness obviously shared by both Columba and Comgall at this inter-communal strife:

Another time, after the convention of the kings at the Ridge of Ceate (Druim Ceatt) . . . the blessed man returned to the sea-coast, and on a calm day in summer he and the Abbot Comgell sat down not far from the above-named fort. Then water was brought in a bronze vessel to the saints from a well that was close by to wash their hands. When St Columba had received the water, he thus spoke to Abbot Comgell, who was sitting at his side, 'A day shall come, O Comgell! when the well whence this water now poured out for us was drawn will be no longer fit for man's use.' 'How?' said Comgell; 'shall the water of this spring be defiled?' 'From this,' said St Columba, 'that it shall be filled with human blood; for thy relatives and mine – that is, the people of the Cruithni and the race of Niall – shall be at war in the neighbouring fortress of Cethirn. Whence, at this same well, an unhappy relative of mine shall be slain, and his blood, mingling with that of many others, shall fill it up.' This truthful prophecy was duly accomplished after many years . . .[39]

If only the veil of history could be lifted to allow us to know more about the friendship between these two great Ulstermen, divided by background, yet united in purpose and friendship. A poem attributed to Columba reads:

feis ac Comgall, cuairt co Caindech,
robad mellach.

[to pass the night with Comgall, to visit Cainnech – how pleasant that would be.] [40]

Surely the friendship of these two great personages from Ulster's past possesses an unambiguous message for the tragically-divided communities of present-day Northern Ireland.

The legend of Columba would have us believe that it was the political and ethnic distractions prevalent within Ulster, from which he himself had not been immune, which finally persuaded him to leave Ireland and set up a new community out of sight of its shores. As J T Fowler wrote:

It is no marvel then if Columba, a leading spirit in the great clan of the northern Uí Néill, incited his kinsmen to fight about matters which would be felt most keenly as closely touching their tribal honour. But at the same time, such a man as he was may very well, upon calm reflection, have considered that his enthusiasm and energies would be more worthily bestowed on missionary work than in maintaining the dignity of his clan.[41]

Whatever the reasons for Columba's departure, the history of the Church was to be much the richer, for the community he founded, on the small island of Iona, close to the coast of Argyll, was destined to be the cultural apotheosis of Scotland.

The Ulster-Scottish Connection

When Columba made his landfall on Iona not all the inhabitants of nearby Argyll would have been strangers to him. As a possible consequence of Uí Néill territorial gains, groups from Ulster had begun to move across the North Channel, in particular a branch of the Ulaid, the Dál Riata, who held territory in the north-eastern part of Antrim, called Dalriada (and which, according to the ancient annals, was separated from the Cruthin kingdom of Dalaradia by the Ravel River in Glenravel). The Dál Riata were the most prominent in settling Argyll and the islands along the western seaboard of what became Scotland (named so after the Ulster settlers, whom the Romans had collectively called 'Scotti'). The kings of Dál Riata soon claimed sovereignty over territory on both sides of the North Channel and when Fergus MacErc forsook his Irish capital of Dunseverick around 500 and established his main residence in Argyll, we must assume that by this time the Scottish colony had superseded the mother-country in importance.

One writer has suggested that Columba's own countrymen, the 'Scots' of Dalriada, might have begun to lapse from the church, and 'the real reason for his leaving Ireland in the first place could well have been to undertake a missionary journey to recall people to the true faith.'[42]

Argyll was not the only part of Scotland to bear witness to an 'Ulster connection'. The history of Christianity in Scotland effectively starts with the settlement established by St Ninian at Candida Casa (now Whithorn) in Galloway in 397 AD. The proximity of Galloway to Ulster meant that evangelism was easily carried across the North Channel. Finnian, who founded the religious community at Moville on Strangford Lough in County Down, had been a student at Candida Casa. He may have been British in speech, as his original name Uinnian implies.[43] The church at Bangor would also have had strong links with this area; indeed, a Bangor monk became Abbot of Candida Casa at the end of the sixth century and churches in Galloway were often dedicated to saints popular in Ulster.

Aside from the evidence of this ecclesiastical 'exchange', there also appears to be strong evidence for a population movement across the North Channel to Galloway. As Charles Thomas wrote:

> An admirable guide to the early Irish settlement could be constructed from the distribution of certain place-name elements – particularly those relating to simple natural features. [Such place-name elements are found in] an intense localized concentration in the double peninsula of the Rhinns of Galloway, opposite Antrim. No special historical sources describe what now looks like another early Irish colony here – possibly of the sixth century. But isolated archaeological finds from Galloway, the spread of a type of early ecclesiastical site (the enclosed developed cemetery) which may be regarded as Irish-inspired, and several minor pointers in the same direction, are mounting to reliable evidence for a separate settlement in this south-eastern area.[44]

For some reason certain academics are quick to belittle any suggestion that the Cruthin would have played much part in these population movements across the North Channel. Richard Warner wrote that 'if any Cruithin at all were involved in the settlements of Scotland they were a tiny minority and are not recorded.'[45] However, irrespective of not having had their history 'recorded' for the benefit of future historians, it does seem highly improbable that a people reckoned to form 'the bulk of the population'[5] in the reduced over-kingdom of Ulster, would not have played a significant part in any movements across to Scotland.

Certainly, a movement of the Cruthin to Galloway would help make sense of certain historical references which have long troubled historians. For example, at the battle of the Standard (1138), the Scottish King David had under his command, according to an English chronicler, 'an army of Normans, Germans, English, of Northumbrians and Cumbrians, of men of Teviotdale and Lothian, of Picts who are commonly called Galwegians and of Scots.' Furthermore, the Galwegians were taunted by English shouts of 'Irish, Irish!' as they joined battle. As W A Hanna pointed out:

> . . . the Picts of Galloway figure prominently in old historical works. [Some] modern historians consider the placing of Picts in Galloway by early chronicles as 'an extraordinary error' based on 'mistaken assumptions and unsound conclusions'. It is true that the Romans generally applied the name Pict to the tribes north of the Antonine Wall and the Forth-Clyde line which formed the southern boundary of the later historical Pictish kingdoms. It is also true that there is little linguistic or accredited archaeological evidence of traditional Picts further south. However, it has been shown that the Pictish tribes were of the same Pretanic stocks as the Cruthin of Ireland, so if appreciable numbers of the latter had migrated the short distance from east Ulster to Galloway, the confusion in terminology could readily be understood.
>
> That some such successful settlement of Cruthin

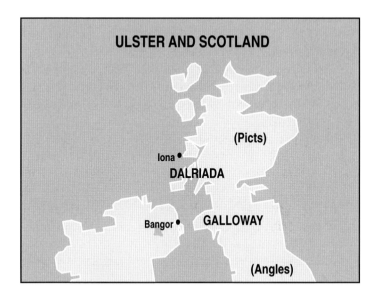

ULSTER AND SCOTLAND

(Picts)

Iona •

DALRIADA

Bangor • GALLOWAY

(Angles)

in Galloway did in fact occur seems to be beyond dispute. [The] old Welsh records, dealing with the northern Brittonic kingdoms as well as with Wales itself, allude to *Gwyddel Ffichti* or 'Irish Picts', [and] old works on the early history of Scotland refer to 'Cruthin or Irish Picts'. In one local regional history Paterson writes of 'Galloway Cruthin', and in another similar work Maxwell records that the 'Galloway Picts' tended to throw in their lot with 'their congeners of Ulster' rather than their neighbours the Strathclyde Britons.[46]

One remarkable piece of evidence is that the word Cruthin survived in the Lowland Scots language as 'Kreenie' well into modern times. Its usage also testifies much to the downward social mobility eventually experienced by the descendants of the original immigrants. As Daphne Brooke points out:

> [The] survival of [great estates] to the very threshold
> of the twelfth century emphasised the strength of the
> Brittonic element in Galloway's medieval culture. . . .
> Great estates required a large work-force [and] were
> probably served by a servile class of Gaelic-speakers.
> Dialect words 'gossok' and 'kreenie', still current in
> the nineteenth century, suggest as much. 'Gossok'
> has been shown to be a survival corresponding to the
> Welsh 'gwasog' which originally implied a person of
> servile status. 'Kreenie' deriving from the Cruithnich
> of northern Ireland, seems to have been a synonym;
> and became a contemptuous word, even a term of
> abuse. Evidently the 'kreenie' had been subject to a
> Welsh-speaking aristocracy who called them
> 'gwasog'.[47]

Significantly, when Galloway re-emerges from historical obscurity in the early twelfth century, after almost three hundred years of silence, the region, according to Peter Hill, 'had been transformed in the intervening period. The shape, size and internal arrangements of the [new] buildings are matched closely at Whiteford, Co. Down, and comparable, though larger, structures have been excavated at Ballywee and Craig Hill, Co. Antrim.'[48]

A strong Ulster element, as evidenced by intrusive Dalaradian souterrain ware, had certainly been added to that alliance of Britons, Northumbrians and Scandinavians which seems to have maintained the independence of the region until the early eleventh century.

Thus did the Ulster Cruthin re-enter history as the 'Picts'* called Galwegians.

---

* The 'Pechts' were to linger on in Ulster-Scots folklore until recent times. See Philip Robinson, 'Picts, Danes and "Broonies" in Ulster-Scots Folklore', *Ullans* 5, 1997.

Columbanus – 'patron saint of Europe'

Another of the great figures of the early Irish Church was Columbanus, born, it was said, of the Leinster Cruthin around the year 543. Like Columba, he too was a close friend of Comgall and remained for many years as Comgall's disciple at Bangor.

In 589 Columbanus set off from Bangor on what was to become one of the great missionary journeys of history. With him he had twelve companions, including his devoted friend, Gall.

The European mainland upon which Columbanus and his party set foot had witnessed traumatic times. The Roman Empire and its system of government had disintegrated under the impact of barbarian invasions, with devastating consequences for the Christian church. Ireland, however, was unaffected by these barbarian incursions – indeed, it had only been indirectly touched by Roman civilisation itself – and the Church and its traditions of learning remained unimpaired.

Arriving in the Merovingian kingdom of Burgundy Columbanus and his companions applied their energies to the establishment of a religious community at Annegray; then, to cope with the flood of recruits, another and even more renowned community was established at nearby Luxeuil. When this second foundation also attracted an increasing number to its brotherhood, a third foundation was necessitated at Fontaine. In fact, Luxeuil was to influence directly or indirectly nearly one hundred other religious foundations before the year 700.

The rules drawn up for these communities were no doubt

modelled on the *Good Rule of Bangor* written by Comgall. They covered everything from timetables for the recitation of psalms to instructions for obedience, fasting, and daily chanting. Some of the régime seems unnecessarily harsh and authoritarian, particularly the use of corporal punishment for infringements of the rules. However, a more insightful approach is also revealed: 'The talkative is to be punished with silence, the restless with the practice of gentleness, the gluttonous with fasting, the sleepy with watching, the proud with imprisonment, the deserter with expulsion.'

Conflict with the secular rulers led to Columbanus' banishment from his beloved monastery, and he journeyed, by a circuitous 600-mile route, to Bregenz, which lies in present-day Austria, close to the borders with Switzerland and Germany. Here Columbanus and his companions began again – building a small cloistered monastery, laying out a garden and planting fruit trees. The local people, however, resentful of these intruders who had the effrontery to smash their pagan images and throw them into the nearby lake, forced Columbanus to uproot himself yet again.

Although by now more than seventy years of age, Columbanus crossed the snow-covered Alps through St Gothard's Pass and made his way to the court of the Lombard king, who granted him a suitable location, at Bobbio, to establish a new monastery. Columbanus was to die a year later but Bobbio was to grow in stature, attracting some of the finest scholars of the time and containing a splendid library of over 700 books.

G S M Walker has written of Columbanus:

> A character so complex and so contrary, humble and haughty, harsh and tender, pedantic and impetuous by turns, had as its guiding and unifying pattern the ambition of sainthood. All his activities were

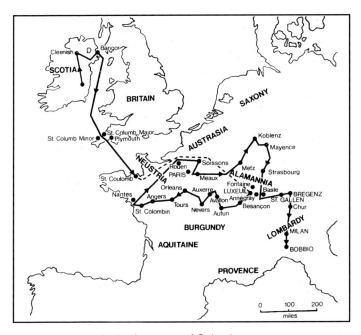

In the footsteps of Columbanus

subordinate to this one end and with the self-sacrifice that can seem so close to self-assertion he worked out his sole salvation by the wondrous pathway that he knew. He was a missionary through circumstance, a monk by vocation, a contemplative, too frequently driven to action by the world, a pilgrim on the road to Paradise.[49]

Many have acknowledged the significance of Columbanus and his fellow missionaries. Pope Pius XI has said: 'The more light that is shed by scholars in the period known as the Middle Ages the clearer it becomes that it was thanks to the initiative and labours of Columbanus that the rebirth of Christian virtue and civilisation over a great part of Gaul, Germany and Italy took place.' The French poet Leon Cathlin wrote: 'He is, with Charlemagne, the greatest figure of our Early Middle Ages,' and Daniel-Rops of the French Academy has said that he was 'a sort of prophet of Israel, brought back to life in the sixth century, as blunt in his speech as Isaias or Jeremias. . . For almost fifty years souls were stirred by the influence of St Columbanus. His passing through the country started a real contagion of holiness.' More recently, Robert Schuman, the French Foreign Minister who was a driving force behind the establishment of the European Economic Community, said: 'Columbanus is the patron saint of those who seek to construct a united Europe.'

And of course the debt owed by Europe to Bangor remained undiminished. Such was the veneration in which it was held that in the twelfth century St Bernard of Clairvaux wrote:

> A place it was, truly sacred, the nursery of saints who brought forth fruit most abundantly to the Glory of God, insomuch that one of the sons of that holy congregation, Molua by name, is alone reputed to have been the founder of a hundred monasteries: which I mention for this reason, that the reader may, from this single instance, form a conception of the number to which the community amounted. In short, so widely had its branches extended through Ireland and Scotland that these times appear to have been especially foreshadowed in the verses of David:
>
>> 'Thou visitest the earth and waterest it; thou greatly enrichest it; the river of God is full of water; thou preparest them corn when thou hast so provided for it. Thou waterest the ridges thereof abundantly; thou makest it soft with showers; thou blessest the springing thereof.'
>
> Nor was it only into the countries I have mentioned but even into distant lands that crowds of saints, like

an inundation, poured. One of whom, St Columbanus, penetrating into these our regions of France, built the monastery of Luxeuil and there became a great multitude. So great do they say it was that the solemnisation of divine offices was kept up by companies, who relived each other in succession so that not for one moment, day or night, was there an intermission of their devotions.

This great period of Irish missionary energy was significant not only for the religious impact it had upon Europe, but because of its importance to the development of European learning in general. As one modern encyclopedia noted, 'the influence of the Irish on European culture can hardly be overemphasized,'[50] a point also made by the German Celtic scholar Heinrich Zimmer:

They were the instructors in every branch of science and learning of the time, possessors and bearers of a higher culture than was at that time to be found anywhere on the Continent, and can surely claim to have been the pioneers – to have laid the cornerstone of western culture on the Continent.[51]

Just as significantly, this upsurge of learning and scholarship went hand in hand with a remarkable artistic outpouring, best epitomised by the beautiful 'illuminated manuscripts' painstakingly compiled in the *scriptoria* of the monasteries, such as the magnificent *Book of Kells*, believed to have been executed at Iona.

Drawing upon the traditional art of their pagan past, Irish monks decorated their great manuscript books and the accoutrements of their churches with designs that are a breathtaking reminder of the art of their forebears . . . Margins overflow with patterns of swirling, interlocking lines, and entire pages are given over to scriptural pictures that are a kaleidoscope of colour and restless patterns. Perhaps the most famous of these Bible pages are the dazzling 'carpet pages', covered in their entirety with patterns that rival the delicacy of the finest metalwork and the brilliance of enamel or precious stones.[52]

The Cradle of Irish Literature

While this flowering of culture had spread outwards to the European mainland from Ireland, Bangor was to play just as significant a role in the flowering of indigenous culture, particularly in the field of literature. As Proinsias Mac Cana wrote:

> In Ireland the seventh century was marked by two closely related developments: the rapid extension of the use of writing in the Irish language and an extraordinary quickening of intellectual and artistic activity which was to continue far beyond the limit of the century. The immediate sources of this artistic renewal were the scriptoria of certain of the more progressive monasteries and its direct agents those monastic literati whom the Irish metrical tracts refer to by the significant title of *nualitride*, 'new men of *letters*'. While there is no reason to suppose that these individuals were confined to any one part of the country, nevertheless the evidence strongly suggests that it was only in the east, or more precisely in the south-east, of Ulster that their activities assumed something of the impetus and cohesiveness of a cultural movement. Here conservation and creativity went hand in hand: the relatively new skill of writing in the vernacular began to be vigorously exploited not only for the direct recording of secular oral tradition – heroic, mythological and the more strictly didactic – but also at the same time as a vehicle for the

> imaginative re-creation of certain segments of that tradition, so that one may with due reservations speak of this region of south-east Ulster as the cradle of written Irish literature. . . . Bangor seems to have been the intellectual centre whence the cultural dynamic of the east Ulster region emanated.[53]

Mac Cana felt that one of the most obvious reasons behind this intellectual and artistic flowering was the geographical position of east Ulster.

> The explanation for all this is not far to seek. It is almost axiomatic that isolation tends towards stagnation, or at least to a circumscribed vision, while conversely intercourse and cultural commerce encourage a greater intellectual curiosity and awareness, a greater readiness to adapt old ways and experiment with new ones. For such intercourse the east-Ulster region was ideally situated. It was a normal landing-place for travellers from northern Britain, which during the sixth and seventh centuries probably presented a more dramatic clash and confluence of cultures than any other part of Britain or Ireland; and, in addition, the religious, social and political ties that linked north-eastern Ireland and north-western Britain – particularly in that period – were numerous and close. Archaeologists speak of an 'Irish Sea culture-province' with its western flank in Ireland and its eastern flank in Britain; one might with comparable justification speak of a North Channel culture-province within which obtained a free currency of ideas, literary, intellectual and artistic.[53]

For far too long Northern Ireland has been viewed by many as the place where antagonistic traditions of Britishness and Irishness most sharply come into conflict. Yet there is no reason whatsoever why we cannot turn that perception completely on its head, and view Northern Ireland as the place where a new symbiosis between these two aspirations could be engendered – just as seemed to have occurred in the sixth and seventh centuries. The people of Northern Ireland, even if many in both communities do not always wish to acknowledge the fact, are *already* the product of such a cross-fertilisation. We in Northern Ireland are a very fortunate people; the marvellous diversity of both Irish and British culture has been accorded to us, and we should all be proud of what we are – one of the most ancient peoples of Western Europe.[54]

The Ulster Tales

At Bangor were compiled in all probability the original Chronicles of Ireland, and the ancient 'Ulster Chronicle' – from which it is believed the oldest entries in the *Annals of Ulster* were derived – has been attributed to Sinlan Moccu Min, who is described in the lists of abbots in the *Bangor Antiphonary* as the 'famed teacher of the world'.

In this region too the ancient traditions of Ulster were preserved, some of which were moulded into the Gaelic masterpiece, the *Táin Bó Cuailgne* (Cattle Raid of Cooley), part of the collection of tales referred to as 'The Ulster Cycle'. The Ulster Cycle depicts a time, generally thought to be the first few centuries AD, when the territory of Ulster encompassed the entire north of Ireland. As has already been noted, when the Cycle was first committed to writing – the language of the earliest form of the *Táin* is dated to the eighth century, though some of the verse passages may be two centuries older – ancient Ulster had greatly contracted, and the Ulstermen – the Ulaid and Cruthin – were confined east of the River Bann, while the Uí Néill dominated the remainder of their former territory.

In the seventh and eight centuries the abbots of Bangor were still generally drawn from the Dál nAraidi, from whom had come the monastery's founder, Comgall. The monastery itself was located within the political sphere of the Dál Fiatach, and it is easy to assume that the literati from both groups wished to propagate stories extolling Ulster's glorious past, with perhaps some regret that that past was no more. Some scholars have detected a hint of such concerns even in those stories which deal with mythology or the mysterious realms of the imagination.

> As well as the literary convention that the Otherworld, even under water or underground, appears as a mirror image of ordinary life, historical changes of ownership could also make lands once known intimately accessible no longer. Stories of lost territories seem to play an important role in the early literature of Ulster.[55]

Later, when the balance of power had moved irrevocably against the Ulstermen, writers began to reflect the new political reality more assertively, as when one eleventh-century scribe added the following comment to his transcription: 'these stories did not happen at all as they were told, but it was to ingratiate themselves with the rude Ulster race that the smooth-tongued poets invented the lying fables.'

Although the Gaelic dynasties, particularly the Uí Néill, eventually came to dominate politics in Ulster – even if it would not be until the fourteenth century that they could finally make good their claim to be rulers of the entire province – nevertheless, as Douglas Hyde remarked, they never sought to identify themselves with the chief protagonists of the Ulster Cycle, the warrior band known as the 'Heroes of the Red Branch'.

> It is worth noting that none of the Gaelic families trace their pedigree, so far as I know, to either Cuchulain himself, or to his over-lord, King Conor mac Nessa. If Irish pedigrees had been like modern ones for sale, or could in any way have been tampered with, everyone would have preferred Cuchulain for an ancestor. That no one has got him is a strong presumption in favour of the genuineness of Irish genealogies.[56]

Somewhat more surprisingly, among the main groups who comprised the Ulster confederacy, there seems to have been a similar consensus – with 'ownership' of the Ulster tales being conceded to the Cruthin rather than to their main rivals, the Ulaid.

Indeed, seemingly concerned by the confusion which might arise because the Ulaid (whose most dominant dynasty were the Dál Fiatach) had also given their name to the actual territory of Ulster (which, of course, embraced areas controlled by Cruthin as well as Ulaid dynasties), the ancient genealogists pointed out that although the Dál Fiatach might be *called* the 'Ulaid', they were not the 'true' Ulaid, but a people of Érainn origin who happened to reside 'in the land of the Ulaid'. According to the genealogists: 'The true Ulaid are Dál nAraidi who spring from Connall Cernach.' As Margaret Dobbs noted:

> The genealogies in nearly every instance assert the Munster origin of Dál Fiatach. How and when do they appear in Ulster? The traditions embodied in the saga of the Táin Bo Cuailgne do not mention them. As they became eventually the over-lords of the Dál Araidi they might have sought a place in the great epic, but this is not the case. The whole glory of the Táin is left to the Dál Araidi whose ancestors are the heroes of that great war. The Dál Fiatach stuck to the claim that they were of the same stock as the Erainn of Kerry, whose greatest hero was Cu Roi, the opponent of the Ulaid of the Táin.[57]

Although a couple of genealogical texts *do* link the Dál Fiatach with King Conchobar, the prevailing view of the ancient genealogists, as Kay Muhr points out, was to make the primary link to the Cruthin, through a 'fictitious' character called Rudraige who was made the ancestor of all the Ulster Cycle heroes:

> Thus the Ulster Cycle became more and more
> associated with the Cruthin. . . . It is extraordinary
> that this one-sided appropriation of the ancient name
> Ulaid was not effectively resisted. . . . In their claim
> to unique descent from Rudraige, and the expansion
> of the theory from the genealogies into the Ulster
> Cycle tales, *Dál nAraide* must have had powerful
> backing: under pressure from west and south in the
> 8th century they would not have had the power to
> support these assertions on their own.[55]

Some present-day academics, strangely antagonistic to the
Cruthin, go to great lengths to denigrate any prominence attached
to them, either in terms of the politics of the day or in the
linkage to the Ulster sagas. For example, Richard Warner
complained:

> The Cruthin are rather minor, and they are rather
> unimportant and they made very little influence on
> Irish power or politics. One of the [current] claims
> made . . . is that the Cruthin were the main people of
> the north and that their hero was Cúchulainn and they
> had their capital at Navan. This is an absolutely gross
> misreading even of the confused early history as far
> as we can interpret it.[58]

Ironically, the prominence accorded to the Cruthin is not
dependant on any present-day 'misreadings', but arises directly
from the writings of the ancient historians and genealogists
themselves. And as for Cúchulainn, I believe that he may have
had his origins in the ancient British tribe, the Setantii.

Irrespective of the real connection, and, indeed, irrespective of
whether the tales which make up the Ulster Cycle are pure
myth or whether they do embody genuine aspects of early
Ulster history, they nevertheless stand as a vital ingredient of

early Irish literature. Some of the tales have become well known to a modern audience, partly because of an increasing popularisation of the ancient texts, and partly because many great Irish literary figures and political activists of modern times have drawn inspiration from the remarkable characters contained within them: the mighty Cúchulainn, the 'Hound of Ulster'; the tragic 'Deirdre of the Sorrows'; the formidable if ruthless Queen Maeve; the brooding and at times vindictive King Conor; the vengeful Connall Cernach; the tragic Ferdia.

The *Táin Bó Cuailgne* is the masterpiece of Irish saga literature. Indeed, it is the oldest story written in the vernacular in Western European literature, thus placing the importance of the East Ulster literary renaissance within a European context as well as making it pivotal to the birth of written Irish literature. The following brief synopsis does but scant justice to this great epic of Irish literature.

*   *   *   *   *

Táin Bó Cuailgne

Queen Medb (Maeve) set out with a great army, composed of the 'men of Ireland'. It was her intention to plunder and lay waste the lands of the Ulaid and the Cruthin as far north as Dún Sobairche (Dunseverick), while the men of Ulster were suffering from their sickness.

It was on the same day that Cúchulainn and his father arrived at the pillar-stone at Ard Cuillenn. As they let their horses graze, Cúchulainn spoke thus to his father: 'I have a premonition that an army is nearby. The least that one who is guarding the border can do is raise the alarm that the enemy is at hand, so go quickly to warn the Ulstermen.' While his father set off, Cúchulainn kindled a fire and remained on guard.

He soon saw the men of Ireland pitch their camp, and over their heads he saw the fiery glitter of the bright gold weapons while the sun set among the evening clouds. Anger and rage filled him at the sight of the multitude of his foes. He brandished his spear, waved his sword, and uttered a hero's cry from his throat.

Cúchulainn engaged the men of Ireland single-handedly until a great dejection and weariness took possession of him. His father, hearing of this, once again climbed onto the rampart at Emain Macha and repeatedly cried out: 'Men are being slain, women carried off, cattle driven away, O Ulstermen!'

King Conchobor (Conor) finally raised himself from his trance and his sickness, ordered that the men of Ulster be assembled and mustered, and declared: 'As the sky is above us, the earth beneath us and the sea all around us, I swear that unless the sky with all its stars should fall upon the earth, or the ground burst open in an earthquake, or the sea sweep over the land, we shall never retreat one inch, but shall gain victory in battle and return every women to her family and every cow to its byre.'

As Queen Medb and Fergus and many noblemen of Ireland scanned the plain, they saw a great grey mist which filled the void between heaven and earth, with what seemed like sifted snow drifting down, above which flew a multitude of birds, and all this accompanied by a great clamour and uproar.

Fergus turned to Medb. 'The grey mist we see is the fierce breathing of the horses and the heroes, the sifted snow is the foam and froth being cast from the horses' bits, and the birds are the clods of earth flung up by the horses' dashing hooves.'

'It matters little,' said Medb, 'we have good warriors with which to oppose them.'

'I wouldn't count on that,' replied Fergus, 'for I assure you that you won't find in all Ireland or Alba (Scotland) a host which can oppose the Ulstermen once their fits of wrath come upon them.'

At the end of the battle all the men of Ireland were routed westwards over the hill. Fergus surveyed the retreating army: 'This host has been destroyed today because we allowed ourselves to be led into disaster by a misguided woman.'[59]

'The Voyage of Bran'

When a professor of Dublin University once denigrated ancient Irish literature by asserting that it contained 'absolutely nothing that in the faintest degree rivals the splendour of the vernacular literatures of the Middle Ages' in the rest of Europe, Douglas Hyde was moved to respond:

> I should be glad if he were to institute a comparison between 'the splendours of the vernacular literatures' of Germany, England, Spain and even Italy and France, prior to the year 1000, and that of the Irish, for I am very much mistaken if in their early development of rhyme, alone, in their masterly treatment of sound, and in their absolutely unique and marvellous system of verse-forms, the Irish will not be found to have created for themselves a place alone and apart in the history of European literatures.[56]

In Hyde's opinion, one such example of this literary brilliance was the 'voyage-tale' *Immram Brain maic Febail* – the Voyage of Bran Son of Febal – possibly written in the eighth century and not later than the ninth.

> I know of few things in literature comparable to this lovely description, at once so mystic and so sensuous, of the joys of the otherworld. To my mind it breathes the very essence of Celtic glamour, and is shot through and through with the Celtic love of form, beauty, landscape, company, and the society of woman.[56]

While, as we have seen, 'ownership' of the Ulster Cycle is said to have been 'appropriated' by the Dál nAraidi, there is no uncertainty with regard to their ownership of the story of Bran. In the course of Bran's voyage to the Otherword, the God Manannán appears, announcing the birth of the historical Dál nAraidi prince, Mongán son of Fiachna (about whom a separate cycle of tales exists, one of which, *Compert Mongáin*, is closely related to a passage in *Immram Brain*).

> The tales of Mongán and Bran are exceptional in that they constitute a sort of minor cycle belonging peculiarly to Bangor and Dál nAraidi: no doubt many other tales passed into Irish literature via Bangor that do not bear such clear internal evidence of the fact.[53]

In the following synopsis the verse sections are taken, initially, from Kuno Meyer's translation.[70]

*   *   *   *   *

The Voyage of Bran

One day Bran, son of Febal, was wandering alone not far from the royal household when he heard music coming from behind him. However, no matter which way he turned, the music still seemed to be behind him. Then he felt himself become drowsy, and the sweetness of the music soon lulled him into a deep sleep. When he awoke he discovered lying beside him a branch of pure silver, arrayed with white blossoms. Mystified, Bran carried the branch into the royal house, and then, to the surprise of all who were gathered there, a woman clad in strange raiment suddenly materialised before them. She was obviously of the *sídh*, the fairy realm, and she began to describe to Bran the delights of a distant 'land of wonders', an island paradise full of light, colour and everlasting joy, peopled by beautiful women, and in which was found neither sickness, sorrow nor death.

Unknown is wailing or treachery
In the familiar cultivated land,
There is nothing rough or harsh
But sweet music striking on the ear.

A beauty of a wondrous land,
Whose aspects are lovely,
Whose view is a fair country,
Incomparable is its haze.

It is a day of lasting weather
That showers silver on the lands,
A pure-white cliff on the range of the sea,
Which from the sun receives its heat.

The mysterious woman then urged Bran to set sail at once for this enchanted land.

Do not fall on a bed of sloth,
Let not thy intoxication overcome thee,
Begin a voyage across the clear sea,
If perchance thou mayst reach the land of women.

Suddenly the branch, which Bran had been holding all the while, sprang from his grasp and into the hand of the woman, who thereupon disappeared as mysteriously as she had appeared. Bran wasted little time assembling a crew and the following dawn he put to sea. When he and his companions had been voyaging for two days they saw a chariot approaching over the waves. Its single occupant made himself known to them, proclaiming that he was Manannán, the son of Lir. He too extolled the virtues of the travellers' destination, describing what Bran would find when he reached it.

The size of the plain, the number of the host,
Colours glisten with pure glory,
A fair stream of silver, cloths of gold,
Afford a welcome with all abundance.

A beautiful game, most delightful,
They play (sitting) at the luxurious wine,
Men and gentle women under a bush,
Without sin, without crime.

Along the top of a wood has swum
Thy coracle across ridges,
There is a wood of beautiful fruit
Under the prow of thy little skiff.

A wood with blossom and fruit,
On which is the vine's veritable fragrance,
A wood without decay, without defect,
On which are leaves of golden hue.

During this recounting Manannán also foretold of the part he himself would play in the birth of the Dál nAraidi prince, Mongán, son of Fiachna, prophesying however that eventual bloodshed would fall upon the Dál nAraidi household. [The verses are now taken from an unpublished rendition by Belfast Shankill Road poet Denis Greig.]

The great Mannanán, descendant of Lir,
Shall be permitted to be a vigorous bed-fellow to
    Caintigern.
I shall call forth my son to this beautiful world
And he shall be acknowledged by Fiachna as his
    own.

He'll have the affection and good company of all
    the *sídh*,
He'll be the darling of every good land;
He'll understand mysteries and be rich in wisdom;
He'll live without fear.

Though he will be seen to be possessed of many
    blessings

During his many fair years of kingship;
The slopes of his land will become grave-strewn;
Sadness will drip into watercourses running red,
And chariot wheels will cut a path around his
    noble dwelling.

Though his kingship will be surrounded by
    champions
And fierce warriors shall guard him closely;
Into his strongholds high over the land,
An end to him shall be sent from Islay.*

Bran and his companions continued their voyage until they
eventually reached the island of women. Even though some of
the women were calling out invitingly from the shore, Bran was
still hesitant to make a landing. Suddenly the leader of the
women threw a ball of thread straight towards Bran's face.
Instinctively he raised his hand to protect himself and the ball
stuck fast to his palm. Almost effortlessly the woman wound in
the thread and the boat was pulled inexorably to the shore. For
Bran and his companions it was the beginning of their long
sojourn in paradise.

At last on shore at their journey's end
In this fabulous land all Time they'd spend;
Each had his bed and bedmate too
And indulged in whatever they wished to do.

Of food, no matter how much they ate,
It never diminished from off the plate,

---

* The *Annals of Tigernach* record that 'Mongan mac Fiachna Lurgan
was struck with a stone by Artuir (Arthur) son of Bicour the Briton
and died.' A verse follows:
    Cold is the wind over Islay;
    there are warriors in Kintyre,
    they will commit a cruel deed therefor,
    they will kill Mongan, son of Fiachna.

And every flavour, about which they enquired,
Was granted as soon as their hearts desired.

To Bran and his crew of three times nine,
Was given enjoyment of women and wine;
The time it passed as a flashing dream
And a century sped as a year it seemed.

Yet, despite this luxurious and carefree lifestyle homesickness eventually overcame one of Bran's companions – Nechtan, son of Collbran. His kin entreated Bran to return to Ireland, but when the leader of the women learned of this she warned them that to return would only bring great unhappiness. However, Bran and his companions eventually resolved to depart, though as they were taking their final leave they were warned never to set foot on dry land.

At last the voyagers sighted Ireland again, and even while approaching shore they engaged in excited conversation with people gathered there. To their dismay no-one on the shore had ever heard of them, although some recalled reading about the 'Voyage of Bran' in their ancient stories. It was only then that they understood that they been in a land where time had lost all meaning.

Suddenly Nechtan, his homesickness making him impatient to touch his homeland once more, leapt into the surf and waded to the beach. To everyone's horror, the instant he reached dry land he turned into a heap of ashes, as though he had been dead for hundreds of years. Bran, recalling the warning they had been given, realised that none of the rest of his party could ever leave the safety of their boat. He called out to the gathering on the shore, giving them details of his voyage, even writing some of it in Ogham for them, then he bade them farewell. And from that hour onwards his wanderings are not known.

But there at the gathering on the shore,
Not one of the people had they seen before.
'Who is it comes over the sea?' asked they;
'Comes over Manannán's field of spray?'

'I'm Bran mac Febal, I've come back here,
I've journeyed far this swift-sped year.'
'We know not a one', spoke up a man,
'Though we've heard a tale called *Immram Bran*.'

Now he named Nectan mac Collbran,
Leapt from the boat onto the land,
The warning forgot! Being head-hot rash
That foolish man's now a heap of ash!
For great is the folly of any man,
Who against his time dares lift a hand.

To all those strangers gathered there,
Bran told of his wanderings everywhere,
This tale in Ogham script he wrote,
Then to sea once more turned his boat.
Now Bran's last words were a brief farewell
And of his wanderings since no man can tell.

*   *   *   *   *

Immram Brain maic Febail was one of the earliest of the
immrama or 'voyage tales', one of which, *Navigatio Sancti
Brendani Abbatis* ('Voyage of St Brendan') was to become
'one of the most influential texts of the Middle Ages ... St
Brendan's Island found its way onto the world map of the
Middle Ages, being claimed by the throne of Spain and sought
by many seafarers.'[61] Christopher Columbus himself knew the
Navigatio. As Alfred Nutt commented:

Of all classes of ancient Irish mythic fiction this is the most famous and the one which has most directly affected the remainder of West European literature. For the Voyage of Saint Brendan, which touched so profoundly the imagination of mediaeval man, which was translated into every European tongue, which drove forth adventurers into the Western Sea, and was one of the contributory causes of the discovery of the New World – the Voyage of Saint Brendan is but the latest and a definitely Christian example of a *genre* of story-telling which had already flourished for centuries in Ireland, when it seemed good to an unknown writer to dress the old half-Pagan marvels in orthodox monkish garb, and thus start them afresh on their triumphal march through the literature of the world.[60]

Congal Cláen and the Battle of Moira

Congal Cláen, undoubtedly the greatest of all Cruthin kings, and attached by the genealogists to the dominant Dál nAraidi dynasty, became over-king of Ulster in 627. Cláen (or Caech) means 'half-blind', and an ancient law-tract on bees preserves a judgement, involving Congal Cláen, concerning recompense due for damages caused by bee-stings. This states that the man who owns the bees should bear the responsibility for any injury:

> *Air is sí cétnae breth inso cet-ara-chét im chinta bech for Congal Cáech cáechsite beich, bach rí Temro conid-dubart assa fhlaith.*

> [For this was the first judgement ever pronounced concerning the crimes of bees against Congal Cáech whom bees blinded; and he was king of Tara until it put him out of his sovereignty.]

This mention of Congal's kingship of Tara in the law-tract is a clear indication that the Ulstermen were far from being a spent force; as Byrne noted:

> This is the only reference in the law-texts to Tara. And it runs directly contrary to the accepted doctrine that it was a monopoly of the Uí Néill. . . . When we remember that the Ulaid and Cruthin were still powerful in county Londonderry and possibly still ruled directly in Louth as far as the Boyne in the early seventh century; that they cherished memories of their former dominance over all the North; that they

considered the Uí Néill recent upstarts; that they had good prospects of restoring the balance by calling on the original loyalties of their quondam sub-kingdom of Dál Riata: it is not difficult to imagine that they could with some justice lay claim to Tara.[5]

In 628 Congal slew Suibne Menn, the Uí Néill high-king, but was in turn defeated by the Uí Néill successor at Dún Ceithirn in Derry two years later. Dissension among the Uí Néill, however, allowed Congal a respite and he fled to Scotland, where he began to make more strenuous efforts to prepare for the inevitable confrontation.

By 637 Congal had managed to gather around him a powerful army, which included not only his Ulstermen, but, according to Colgan, contingents of Picts (Scots), Anglo-Saxons (English) and Britons (Welsh). His huge army joined combat with the Uí Néill army lead by Domnall mac Áedo at the great battle of Mag Roth (Moira) that same year. The battle, as depicted in later Bardic romances, seems to have been a ferocious affair, and as well as the land confrontation it included a naval engagement. The event was recorded by the annalist Tigernach as follows:

AD 637 — The Battle of Magh Rath was fought by Domnall, son of Aed, and by the sons of Aed Slaine (but Domnall at this time ruled Temoria [Tara]) in which fell Congal Caech, king of Uladh and Faelan, with many nobles; and in which fell Suibne, the son of Colman Cuar.

The battle was also mentioned by Adamnan, the eight abbot of Iona, and in the *Chronicon Scotorum*. It is further recorded, under the incorrect year, in the *Annals of the Four Masters*:

AD 634 – The Battle of Magh Rath fought by Domnall son of Aed, and the sons of Aod Slaine, against Congal

Claon, son of Scallan, king of Ulaidh, and many foreigners along with him, were slain.

The battle engendered a bardic saga which Alfred Nutt considered 'one of the most considerable Irish historic romances extant.'[60] Another who was deeply impressed by the ancient romance and the battle of which it told was Sir Samuel Ferguson, born in Belfast in 1810, and who, before going to study law, attended the Belfast Academical Institution where Gaelic was taught. Ferguson was destined to play a major part in the restoration, from the original Irish, of the ancient literature which had been lost to generations brought up and taught in another language. His *Lays of the Western Gael*, published in 1864, included his version of the *Táin Bó Cúailgne* which brought back into circulation the legend of Cúchulainn and Ulster's formidable adversary, Queen Maeve of Connaught. He became president of the Royal Irish Academy in 1882.

But it was the story of Congal which was to inspire what was for Ferguson his greatest work, the epic poem 'Congal', published in 1872. In its preface he wrote:

> The leading incidents of this Poem are derived from the Irish Bardic romance called 'Cath Muighe Rath, or The Battle of Moyra,' with its introductory 'Pre-Tale' of the 'Fleadh Duin-na n-Gedh, or Banquet of Dunangay.' When these pieces were first given to the public, through the patriotic labours of the Irish Archaeological Society, in 1842, they made a strong and lasting impression on my imagination. They seemed to possess, in a remarkable degree, that largeness of purpose, unity and continuity of action which are the principal elements of Epic Poetry, and solicited me irresistibly to the endeavour to render them into some compatible form of English verse.

However, Ferguson was to find the 'inherent repugnancies

too obstinate for reconcilement', and with some regret he abandoned the attempt. However, he had been 'so strongly impressed' by the saga that he could not 'wholly reject it' from his mind, and he therefore penned his own version of it, which he entitled 'Congal' from the chief actor in it. As Ferguson's version is close in many ways to the original, and gives us a feel for both the event and the bardic style of recounting, it will serve our purpose to retell the story of that battle-saga through a synopsis of Ferguson's epic poem.

But before doing so, we shall set the scene for the battle, again in Ferguson's words, quoting from an article of his reviewing Reeves' *Ecclesiastical Antiquities*:

> We are here upon the borders of the heroic field of Moyra, the scene of the greatest battle, whether we regard the numbers engaged, the duration of combat, or the stake at issue, ever fought within the bounds of Ireland. There appears reason to believe that the fight lasted a week; and on the seventh day Congal himself is said to have been slain by an idiot youth, whom he passed by in battle, in scorn of his imbecility. All local memory of the event is now gone, save that one or two localities preserve names connected with it. Thus, beside the Rath of Moyra, on the east, is the hill Cairn-Albanach, the burial-place of the Scottish princes, Congal's uncles; and a pillar-stone, with a rude cross, and some circles engraved on it, formerly marked the site of their resting-place. On the other hand, the townland of Aughnafoskar probably preserves the name of Knockanchoscar, from which Congal's druid surveyed the royal army, drawn up in the plain below, on the first morning of the battle. Ath Ornav, the ford crossed by one of the armies, is probably modernised in Thorny-ford, on the river, at some miles distance. On the ascent to Trummery, in the direction of the woods of Killultagh, to which, we

are told, the routed army fled, great quantities of bones of men and horses were turned up in excavating the line of the Ulster Railway which passes close below the old church.

*   *   *   *   *

Congal Cláen and The Battle of Moira *(with verses by Sir Samuel Ferguson)*

Congal Cláen, over-king of Ulster, was deeply troubled. More than anyone he felt the sufferings and indignities inflicted upon his beloved Ulster by the hand of the upstart Uí Néill. Yet a peace had been brokered between Ulster and the Uí Néill king, Domnall son of Aed, and it was Congal's duty to honour that peace. Even now, as he bid farewell to his beloved Lafinda, an escort of his most trusted warriors awaited him, their task to escort him to a banquet hosted by Domnall at the latter's royal residence at Dunangay.

On went the royal cavalcade, a goodly sight to see,
As westward, o'er the Land of Light, they swept the
    flowery lea;
Each shining hoof of every steed upcasting high behind
The gay green turf in thymy tufts that scented all the
    wind,
While, crossing at the coursers' heads with intersecting
    bounds,
As swift as skimming swallows played the joyous
    barking hounds.
First of the fleet resplendent band, the hero Congal
    rode;
Dark shone the mighty-chested steed his shapely thigh
    bestrode;
Dark, too, at times, his own brow showed that all his
    lover's air

> But mantled with a passing light the gloom of inward
>> care.

That gloom had still not abated when, en route to Dunangay, Congal accepted overnight hospitality offered by some of his Ulster kinsmen. Yet, rather than being able to relax in their warm-hearted company, the poets' praise of Ulster's former glories only served to deepen his depression.

Nevertheless, when he did finally find himself in the presence of his former adversary, he strove to stifle his resentment and to treat his host with due respect and courtesy. However, whether by accident or intent, a grievous insult was offered to Congal and his hard-gained calm rapidly dissolved. Leaping to his feet before the astonished gathering he recounted the many wrongs perpetrated against Ulster by the king of Meath, and informed all present that those wrongs would be righted on the battlefield. Then, grim-faced, he and his Ulstermen angrily mounted their steeds and immediately sped from Dunangay to prepare for war.

> As through the desert of the bards, at coming close of
>> day,
> On this design intent, the King of Ulster took his way;
> Where fell the shadows vast, and grey from crag and
>> spike of stone
> The curling mists began to rise, tidings before him
>> flown
> Of war denounced, had filled the waste with battle-
>> glorying songs.
> And through the dusky glens the Bards, in loud exulting
>> throngs,
> On each side ran, with augury of conquest and renown
> Crowning the champion; [until] untimely night came
>> down.

Before setting off to gather together his armies Congal hurried to the side of his betrothed. Lafinda was consumed by anguish and foreboding, knowing that much communal suffering and grief would now ensue, a reality which her lover with his vengeful determination had pushed far from his concerns. She pleaded with him to reconsider his proposed course of action.

'Yet, oh, bethink thee, Congal, ere war kindles, of the ties
Of nurture, friendship, fosterage; think of the woful sighs
Of widows, of poor orphans' cries; of all the pains and griefs
That plague a people in the path of battle-wagering chiefs.'

Lafinda's heartfelt pleadings were in vain; Congal's honour and that of Ulster had been grievously insulted, leaving him deaf to all entreaties. What made her heartache all the more poignant was that until the moment of Congal's arrival she had been blissfully preoccupied with thoughts of their approaching wedding day.

'Ah me,' she cried. 'What fate is mine! The daughter of a King,
Wooed by a King, and well content to wear the marriage ring;
Who never knew the childish want not granted, nor desire
Of maiden bosom, but good saints and angels would conspire
To bring the innocent wish to pass: who with the streams and flowers,
So happy was I, turned to joy the very passing hours,
From flowery earth and fragrant air, and all sweet sounds and sights
Filling my heart, from morn to eve, with fresh and pure delights –

> Just when, in bloom of life, I said, 'this world is
> wondrous fair,'
> Now in one hour see nothing left, to live for, but
> despair.'

When Domnall, King of Meath, was informed that Congal's hosts were camped close by at Moira, he accepted the coming clash of arms with the same unyielding resolve he and his kin had displayed in their many conquests across the breadth of Ireland.

> Said Domnal, 'While I live and reign, it never shall be
> said
> The hosts of Erin, with the King of Erin at their head,
> Sat in the shelter of a camp, or shunned the open
> ground,
> While foreign foe or rebel King within the realm was
> found.
> And since on Moyra openly their hosts encamp tonight,
> On Moyra openly at dawn shall Erin give them fight.'

And so it came to pass that the destinies of two great armies drew inexorably together, and a terrible bloodletting became irrevocable with each thundering stride of charging men hastening towards their fatal embrace.

> Swiftly they cleared the narrowing space of plain ground
> interposed;
> And, bearing each an even front, from wing to wing
> they closed.
> A shudder at the closing shock thrill'd through the
> grassy plain,
> And all the sedgy-sided pools of Lagan sighed again.
> In balanced scale, in even fight – no thought on either
> side
> Of yielding back – the eager hosts their work of battle
> plied,

Stern, dark, intense, incessant, as forging smiths that
    smite
In order on the stithy head through spark-showers hailing
    white.
And, as when woodsmen to their work, through copse
    and stubble go,
Grasping the supple red-skinned twigs with darting
    bill-hooks, so
With frequent grasp and deadly grip plucked from their
    slippery stand,
They went continual to the earth: the grassy-vestured
    land,
Stamped into dust, beneath them glowed; the clear
    fresh morning air
Vexed with the storm of whirling arms, and tossing
    heads and hair,
Around them reeked; while overhead, in dense
    unwholesome pall,
A sweat-and-blood-engendered mist rose steaming over
    all.
Dire was the front-rank warriors' case; nor, in their
    deadly need,
Did son of father longer think, or friend of friend take
    heed;
But each deemed all the strength and skill his prowess
    could command
But scant enough to serve the need that claimed his
    proper hand;
Fresh hands with deadlier-wielded blades, new foes
    with angrier frown,
Succeeding ceaseless in the front, fast as the old went
    down.
Fed from behind the ranks renewed: from these continual
    fed
The intermediate heaps increased. Still no man turned
    or fled.

Many were the great warriors of Erin and Ulster forced to meet
an untimely destiny. And amid the corpse-strewn battlefield
Congal pressed hard upon the forces of Clan-Conail, led by
their chief, Conal.

> Clan-Conail, now lock close your shields, make fast
>   your battle-front;
> The might, the might of Ulster comes, and Congal
>   gives the brunt.
> And proudly kept thy host their place, oh Conal, till the
>   stroke
> Of Congal's own close-wielded mace a bloody passage
>   broke.
> Then, though your battle-border long had baffled all
>   his best,
> Shield-lock'd and shoulder-riveted, with many a valiant
>   breast
> That burned with Northern valour as courageous as his
>   own,
> Yet before the face of Congal ye were crushed and
>   overthrown,
> Chaff-dispersed and ember-scattered; till the strong
>   fraternal arm
> Of Kindred-Owen reached between, and stayed you
>   further harm.

Yet the Fates were not to side with Congal Cláen, and although
none of the ablest warriors among his foes could best him in
combat, he stayed his hand from killing one particular enemy,
an imbecile youth he dimly recognised amid the fury of the
battle. It was a fatal generosity, for the youth, as Congal strode
past him, suddenly plunged a bill-hook into his stomach. Congal
staggered under the impact but still disdained to kill his assailant.

> Then round his lacerated side he drew his glittering belt,
> Resumed his arms, and stood erect, as though he scarce
>   had felt

The wound that through his vitals was diffusing death
the while;
And said. 'It grieves me, Cuanna, that the weak hands
imbecile
Of one devoid of reason, should have dealt this fatal
blow;
For, that it is a mortal hurt thou'st given me, well I
know:
And well I knew my death to-day at Moyra stood
decreed;
But thought to find my destiny at some other hands,
indeed . . .'

But Congal, conscious that his strength by slow degrees
decayed,
Resolved, while yet his arm had nerve to lift the wearying
blade,
To spend his still-remaining power in one supreme attack,
That Ulster so with victory, though Kingless, might go
back.

As Congal's strength rapidly began to ebb a faintness swam
before his eyes, yet bravely he strove to wield sword and shield
as his foes closed for the final reckoning. Then, just as they
pressed in upon him, an eerie darkness suddenly enveloped the
battlefield, and even as Congal collapsed onto the ground he
felt himself being lifted aloft as if by strong arms.

But, rapt in darkness and in swoon of anguish and
despair,
As in a whirlwind, Congal Claen seemed borne thro'
upper air;
And, conscious only of the grief surviving at his heart,
Now deemed himself already dead, and that his deathless
part
Journeyed to judgement; but before what God's or
demon's seat

Dared not conjecture; though, at times, from tramp of
giant feet
And heavy flappings heard in air, around and
underneath,
He darkly surmised who might be the messenger of
death
Who bore him doomward: but anon, laid softly on the
ground,
His mortal body with him still, and still alive he found.
Loathing the light of day he lay; nor knew nor reck'd
he where;
For present anguish left his mind no room for other
care;
All his great heart to bursting filled with rage, remorse
and shame,
To think what labour come to nought, what hopes of
power and fame
Turned in a moment to contempt; what hatred and
disgrace
Fixed thenceforth irremovably on all his name and
race. . .
Then Congal raised his drooping head, and saw with
bloodshot eyes
His native vale before him spread; saw grassy Collin
rise
High o'er the homely Antrim hills. He groaned with
rage and shame.
'And have I fled the field,' he cried; 'and shall my
hapless name
Become this byeword of reproach? Rise; bear me back
again,
And lay me where I yet may lie among the valiant
slain.'

As from a distance, the voice of one of his most trusted warriors
finally began to penetrate Congal's consciousness, informing

him that it was he who had seized the opportunity offered by the sudden darkness to place the King of Ulster on a chariot and speed him from the battlefield. As Congal endeavoured to raise himself up despite his pain he noticed that another person was approaching, someone whose graceful movements were unmistakable to him. But even as a grieving Lafinda reached down to touch her lover's eyes, a final flicker told her that Congal Cláen, mighty king of Ulster, was dead.[62]

*　　*　　*　　*　　*

Yeats had written of Ferguson that he was 'consumed with one absorbing purpose, the purpose to create an Irish school of literature, and overshadowed by one masterful enthusiasm, an enthusiasm for all Gaelic and Irish things.' Fittingly, Ferguson's final resting place, at Donegore (north-east of Antrim town), is less than a mile from the still visible earthen fort of Rath Mór, the royal seat of the Dál nAraidi kingdom of Dalaradia.

> There can be few places on earth with an air as peaceful as that of the Church of St John at the foot of Donegore Hill. Old trees overlook it and doves flutter about it. In the churchyard is the grave of Sir Samuel Ferguson. . . . Donegore Hill itself is an ancient earthwork. It has not been excavated, and it is thought to cover a passage-grave. Flint arrow-heads are frequently found around the place. Ferguson, that great romantic, is happy no doubt in company with the ancients, on his own ancestral ground.[63]

The battle of Moira, while not resulting in Ulster's final overthrow, certainly ended any hopes the Ulstermen may have entertained of reversing their fortunes and undoing the Uí Néill territorial gains. From then onwards they were to fight a constant but relatively successful rearguard action, and, somewhat ironically, the final eclipse of what remained of ancient Ulster was not to be accomplished by the Uí Néill, but by another set of newcomers who would arrive in Ireland in the twelfth century.

Although Congal's Dál nAraidi kinsmen clearly suffered a severe setback, the implications of defeat were also felt among other sections of the Ulster alliance, in particular the Dál Riata. Prior to the battle Domnall of the Uí Néill had agreed an alliance with Domnall Brecc of the Dál Riata, but Congal, during his flight to Scotland, managed to reverse this, with the result that the Dalriadans fought alongside him at Moira. Congal may have achieved this reversal because of the traditional friendship between Dalaradia and Dalriada, but Congal's defeat proved disastrous for the latter's fortunes. Domnall Brecc's own death in battle four years later in Scotland effectively marked the end of the Scottish-Irish kingdom of Dalriada, and although Domnall Brecc's successors attempted to retain authority over both sides of the North Channel, by the middle of the seventy century the Ulster territory had begun to go its separate way. This eclipse of a previously strong Ulster-Scottish power-base further helped to consolidate Uí Néill dominance in the North of Ireland.

Ecclesiastically, the defeat at Moira meant that the cult of Patrick was removed from Connor to a new power base at Armagh. Patrick's original choice of Armagh in the fifth century had possibly been influenced, as Eoin MacNeill suggested, by the ancient glories of Emain Macha. But when the ancient capital of Ulster had been destroyed, or abandoned, it seems probable that 'Patrick may have retired from Armagh to Downpatrick with his defeated patrons the Ulster kings'.[5] Certainly Uí Néill hagiographers were obviously embarrassed by the saint's death within Ulaid territory at Saul. But now, with such a decisive defeat having been inflicted upon the Ulster forces, the hagiographers' task was made easier.

[In] the interests of Armagh's primatial ambitions the seventh-century hagiographers Muirchú and Tirechán wished to attach Patrick to the new Uí Néill high-kingship and developed the impressive but probably quite artificial legend of his confrontation with Lóeguire son of Niall and his druids at Tara.[5]

'Sweeney's Frenzy'

Closely related to the *Banquet of Dunangay* and the *Battle of Magh Rath* is a third tale – *Buile Suibhne*, or 'Sweeney's Frenzy' – which is in the form of a sequel to the battle, describing the adventures which befell one of its participants, Suibhne Geilt, after he was driven mad by the horrors of that titanic contest. Notwithstanding the extraordinary and fantastical nature of his adventures, Suibhne himself is said to have been a real person. This assertion adds a degree of intrigue, as J G O'Keeffe noted in the introduction to his own translation of the tale:

> When we consider the prominent part assigned to Suibhne in the tale, it is singular that so little is known of him. It is true that his connection with the battle of Magh Rath is mentioned in that early Irish law tract the *Book of Aicill*. He is also named in the Annals of Tigernach, where it is stated that he fell in the battle. He is mentioned in the Acallamh na Senórach in connection with St. Moling and Ros Brocc. He peers now and again, a dim, mysterious figure, out of the pages of one of the romantic accounts of the battle, and at least two Irish poems, both of considerable antiquity, are attributed to him. He is described in the present tale and in the *Battle of Magh Rath* (ed. O'Donovan) as King of Dal Araidhe, but his name does not appear, so far as I am aware, in any of the lists of kings of that territory. In fact, if we are to trust the list given in the Book of Leinster, Congal Claen was king both of Dal Araidhe and Ulaidh at the time

of the battle. Congal fled from Ireland after the battle of Dun Cethirn in 629, and appears to have remained in exiled until he returned to Ireland to fight at Magh Rath in 637. . . . The kingdom of Dal Araidhe, however, was peopled by Cruithni or Irish Picts, and it is not improbable that these people may have chosen Suibhne to act as regent during the absence of Congal. Suibhne is called king, but the word is used loosely in the annals; the designation of lord may have more closely represented the position.[64]

Before attempting to give a synopsis of the tale, it is worth noting some other observations made by O'Keeffe:

Perhaps the outstanding feature of the composition is the extraordinary love of place which it reveals. I venture to say that this is one of the most distinctive features of early Irish literature. It is only necessary to recall in this connection the vast number of compositions which have for subject the origin of place-names. Nor was this love of place a mere convention; I believe it sprang from a very intimate knowledge of the actual place or of the spirit of the place; and I suggest that it will be found on investigation that the descriptions of places given in early Irish literature are in the main accurate.

In one respect the *Buile Suibhne* possesses special interest. Unlike the large mass of early Irish literary remains, it seems to owe but little to traditional lore. Whatever folk-beliefs and superstitions it may enshrine, the tale in its broad outline seems to be largely independent of floating myth, and the theme is treated in a way that is free from the literary conventions of the time. In a word, the *Buile Suibhne* . . . is a sustained literary *tour de force*, and, as such, furnishes an interesting example of the medieval attitude of mind towards literary creation.

*   *   *   *   *

Sweeney's Frenzy (with verses by J G O'Keeffe)

It so happened that one day Suibhne Geilt, king of Dál nAraidi, was surprised to hear the sound of a bell, and when enquiring of its origin was told that it belonged to [Saint] Ronan, who was nearby, marking out the site of a church. Suibhne was furious that the cleric should have the effrontery to do such a thing in his domain and immediately set out with the utmost haste, intending to expel the cleric forthwith from his lands. In an effort to prevent his sudden departure, Suibhne's wife Eorann seized the hem of the fringed, crimson cloak which he wore around him, and it fell to the ground leaving him start naked. Undaunted, or uncaring, Suibhne stormed off in this state, not halting until he encountered Ronan, blithely chanting psalms to the glory of God.

Angrily, Suibhne snatched the psalter from Ronan's hands and flung it into the waters of a nearby lake. He had just laid hands roughly on the cleric when a sudden cry distracted his attention. It originated from a serving man of Congal Claen, who arrived bearing the king's urgent entreaty for Suibhne to fight alongside him at the impending battle of Moira.

Immediately Suibhne departed with the messenger, engrossed in questioning him, while Ronan was left standing by the lakeside, sorrowful at the loss of his precious psalter and fuming over the dishonour which had been inflicted upon him. However, an otter eventually swam over to Ronan carrying the book, and to his joy he found it to be entirely undamaged. He gave thanks to God, but in the same breath cursed Suibhne, saying: 'Be it my will, together with the will of the mighty Lord, that even as he came stark naked to expel me, may it be thus that he will ever be, naked, wandering and flying throughout the world.'

Soon after, the two men again encountered one another at Moira when Ronan and some of his psalmists arrived at the battlefield to sprinkle holy water on the assembled hosts. Suibhne was one of the recipients of this gesture, and, believing that it was being done deliberately to mock him, he slew the nearest psalmist in a fit of rage and even attempted to impale Ronan with his spear. The spear was miraculously deflected and Ronan again invoked his curse on Suibhne.

> Even as in an instant went
> the spear-shaft on high,
> mayst thou go, O Suibhne,
> in madness, without respite!
>
> Thou hast slain my foster-child,
> thou hast reddened thy spear in him,
> thou shalt have in return for it
> that with a spear-point thou shalt die.

In the horrendous din of the battle, which reverberated even up into the clouds above, Suibhne was suddenly overcome by a great unsteadiness and an overwhelming sense of unease. His fingers seemed paralysed, his limbs shook, his heartbeat quickened, his sight became distorted, and finally his weapons fell from his hands. Ronan's curse now fully upon him, Suibhne fled from the battlefield, a stark raving madman.

His feet barely touched the ground as he fled the length and breadth of the countryside, until finally he came to rest in a yew-tree in Glen Earcain, where he tried to conceal himself. It perchanced that some of Suibhne's own kinsfolk, still in flight from their disastrous defeat at Moira, also travelled through that glen, and as they passed below his tree he overheard them enquiring whether he was alive or dead. Suibhne called down to them from his perch.

'O warriors, come hither,
O men of Dal Araidhe,
you will find in the tree in which he is
the man whom you seek.

God has vouchsafed me here
life very bare, very narrow,
without music, without restful sleep,
without womenfolk, without a woman-tryst.

Here at Ros Bearaigh am I,
Ronan has put me under disgrace.
God has severed me from my form,
know me no more, O warriors.

The men urged him to trust them but he refused to listen, and as they closed around the tree Suibhne leaped from it effortlessly and resumed his flight. His next resting place was in a tree in Cell Riagain in Tir Conaill, where this time he found himself in the midst of the victors of the Battle of Moira, King Domnall himself among them. Indeed, it was Domnall who first recognised this strange madman who had suddenly sprung seemingly from nowhere into the tree, and, regretful of the conflict which had risen between himself and Congal's people, he spoke to Suibhne in a praiseworthy and conciliatory tone, endeavouring to entice him to the ground.

'How is that, O slender Suibhne?
thou wert leader of many hosts;
the day the iniquitous battle was fought
at Magh Rath thou wert most comely.

Like crimson or like beautiful gold
was thy noble countenance after feasting,
like down or like shavings
was the faultless hair of thy head.

Like cold snow of a single night
was the aspect of thy body ever;
blue-hued was thine eye, like crystal,
like smooth, beautiful ice.'

But Suibhne was impervious to Domnall's entreaties and as
suddenly as he had appeared in their midst, just as swiftly did
he resume his headlong flight.

And so Suibhne continued his tormented journey throughout
Ireland, searching out the safety and solace of tall trees or
desolate rocky clefts, travelling from peak to peak and from
glen to glen. And at each refuge he hid from his fellow-men,
living in a naked or near-naked state, and constantly bemoaning
his fate.

'Cold is the snow to-night,
lasting now is my poverty,
there is no strength in me for fight,
famine has wounded me, madman as I am.

All men see that I am not shapely,
bare of thread is my tattered garment,
Suibhne of Ros Earcain is my name,
the crazy madman am I.

I rest not when night comes,
my foot frequents no trodden way,
I bide not here for long,
the bonds of terror come upon me.

My goal lies beyond the teeming main,
voyaging the prow-abounding sea;
fear has laid hold of my poor strength,
I am the crazy one of Glen Bolcain.

Seven years Suibhne wandered the Irish countryside, until

finally one of his hiding places was discovered by one of his Dál nAraidi kinsmen, Loingseachan, who managed to approach by donning a woman's garment as a disguise. Suibhne was none too pleased that his current refuge had been revealed, but stayed to talk with Loingseachan, lamenting yet again the curses of Ronan which had driven him to madness.

When the nobles of Dál nAraidi learned that Suibhne's hiding place had been unearthed, they asked Loingseachan to try and entice him back, and hence on the occasion of their next meeting Loingseachan told Suibhne that his father, mother, brother, wife, son and daughter were all dead. So grief-stricken was Suibhne at this news that his madness departed from him and he consented to return with Loingseachan.

Once back among his kin he was informed that his family were in fact all alive, and he was put in the charge of a woman who looked after Loingseachan's mill. She was warned not to speak to him, but she ignored this admonition, and goaded Suibhne into telling her all about his wild life. When he mentioned his feats of flying she urged him to let her see how he accomplished this. He finally agreed, but in attempting to follow him the woman fell to her death, and so Suibhne, in fear of what Loingseachan might do, once more resumed his flight, his madness now fully returned.

More adventures befell Suibhne not only in Ireland but in Britain where he lived for a time with a fellow madman. Although Suibhne intermittently recovered his sanity his madness would invariably return, forcing him to resume his mad flight.

One day, however, he arrived at the place where [Saint] Moling was teaching a group of students. Moling welcomed Suibhne and informed him that not only was his coming there prophesied but also the fact that he would die there. He told Suibhne that no matter how far he might wander during the day, he was to return each night so that his life story could be recorded.

This became the pattern of Suibhne's life for the next year, and each night he would return to his place of rest, where he would be met by Moling's cook who had been instructed to bring him some milk. However, another woman accused the cook of preferring to spend her time looking after the needs of the madman than those of her own husband. When the husband, a herdsman, heard these innuendoes he straightway made for the resting place armed with a spear, and surprising the reclining Suibhne thrust the spear through his breast. Suibhne began his last lament.

> The herd's sharp spear has wounded me,
> so that it has passed clean through my body;
> alas, O Christ, who hast launched every judgement,
> that I was not slain at Magh Rath!

As Suibhne's death-swoon came upon him, Moling, attended by his clerics, arrived and each of them placed a stone on Suibhne's tomb. His tale ends thus: 'So far, some of the tales and adventures of Suibhne son of Colman Cuar, king of Dal Araidhe.'

*   *   *   *   *

Buile Suibhne was to have a lingering impact upon Irish literature:

> Through the story of his wanderings – physical and mental – Suibhne became the principal Irish exponent of the legend of the Wild Man. Many of the motifs attached to him are associated with rites of passage and the transition from one state to another. On the evidence of his encounter with the Scottish madman, as well as analogous traditions in Britain, a remote

British provenance has been posited for the tale. The Suibhne story continues to inspire Irish writers, notably Flann O'Brien in *At Swim-Two-Birds* and Seamus Heaney in *Sweeney Astray*. [61]

The Arthurian Connection

The story of Suibhne Geilt leads us to one final, intriguing aspect of Ulster's literary heritage – its possible connection to the Arthurian legends. Reference has already been made to the fact that Ireland's rich folklore was carried to other parts of Europe, and, in return, European folk tales of all kinds made their way to Ireland. But few bodies of stories have exhibited such a truly 'international' appeal as those comprising the Arthurian literature. When the tales of the deeds of King Arthur and his companions first 'hit' Europe they were a spectacular success; indeed, some clergymen expressed alarm that the populace might prefer the stories of Arthur and his Knights to the teachings of the Church. As Littleton and Malcor noted:

> These vivid tales of love and war, adventure and adultery, piety and betrayal began life as scattered legends in early medieval British chronicles, romances attached to the Welsh *Mabinogion*, and Breton lay (short poems usually narrating a single episode). From these grew one of the most enduring stories ever known, kept alive in our own time by films, plays, operas and novels. Names such as Merlin, Excalibur, Camelot, Morgan le Fay, Tristan, Lancelot and Avalon are still familiar today.[65]

The popular 'craze' began, in literary terms, in the late 1130s with the appearance of *Historia Regum Britanniae* ('The History of the Kings of Britain'), a Latin work by a scholar from Oxford, Geoffrey of Monmouth. His 'history' was a dramatic blending of legend, myth and actual history, and the Arthurian saga thus begun was later developed in the romances of Chrétien de Troyes and his followers. It was a Europe-wide success: firstly, in its composition, for it would eventually draw together stories which had their source in different countries – for example, it was in the French romances that the characters of Lancelot, Perceval, Bors and Galahad were developed – and secondly, in its widespread appeal, for Geoffrey's book was so successful it was adapted and translated all over Europe.

> The tales of Arthur were rendered in every literary and artistic form during the Middle Ages. Chronicles were sober in tone and strove to portray Arthur as a real king. Welsh, Breton and Scottish poets and French and Italian troubadours, however, encompassed humour, satire, horror, romance and fantasy. Storytellers adapted the legends to suit their public: Celts liked tales of magic, the French and Italians enjoyed stories of adultery and courtly love, and the Spanish and Germans preferred the pious legends of the Grail.[65]

The 'stories' relating to Arthur had been in circulation, of course, long before Geoffrey of Monmouth first compiled them. Indeed, there is some evidence for Irish traditions and literature about Arthur which predate Geoffrey's 'History', as the editors of the *Oxford Companion to Irish Literature* point out:

> Early texts of the Fionn cycle make reference to an Arthúr who led a British war-band, while the 11th cent. Irish translation of Nennius' *Historia Brittonum* supplies glimpses of a supposedly historical Arthur. A list of tale-types on the *Book of Leinster* seems to contain a reference to an early Arthurian text, now

lost. The personal name Arthúr occurs several times in early Irish sources, presumably reflecting contact between Irish literature and some branch of the British tradition. The early Irish saga *Scéla Cano meic Gartnáin* has been suggested as a source for the Tristan and Isolde theme later developed in Arthurian romances.[61]

Scholars generally accept that the original Tristan was Drust, son of the Pictish king Talorc, who ruled in northern Britain about 780, and that the legends were later given a new setting in Cornwall. The shape of the legend was then drawn by Welsh writers from the Irish sources, including the tale of Diarmaid and Grainne.

In *The Mystic Dawn* the authors indicate a number of other such linkages:

> Cuchulainn and Gawain are involved in many similar adventures – Cuchulainn, for example, appears in a beheading episode very like the tale of Gawain and the Green Knight – and one theory claims that the two heroes have a common origin, perhaps as a tribal sun-hero of northwestern Britain. . . .
>
> Geoffrey of Monmouth introduced Guinevere as a Roman woman, but her Welsh name, Gwenhyvar, comes from the Irish Finnabair, the daughter of the divine Queen Maeve of Connacht. . . .
>
> The name Morgan [Le Fay] is related to Morrigan, the name of the Irish war goddess [who alighted on the shoulder of the dying Cuchulainn in the form of a crow].[65]

Others have also suggested that King Arthur's Knights of the Round Table were modelled on the Red Branch Knights of Ulster, with Cúchulainn becoming Sir Gawain.

Finally, there is a linkage between the Arthurian tales and the story of Suibhne Geilt. Nikolai Tolstoy, in *The Quest for Merlin*, writes:

> Fortunately it is not necessary to rely solely on deductive analysis ... to show that Geoffrey of Monmouth did not invent the Merlin story, since there is evidence that much of it was already in existence well before his time.[66]

Tolstoy names three other bodies of work as providing such evidence:

> Thus four distinct versions of the prophet's career have survived: the *Vita Merlini* of Geoffrey of Monmouth, the Welsh 'Myrddin' poems, the Lailoken episodes, and the story of Suibhne's frenzy. That they all ultimately represent the same saga (though obviously with accretions and distortions acquired along the way) is abundantly clear and is accepted by the best authorities.[66]

The Politics Continue

While creative and artistic pursuits were establishing Ulster's pre-eminent position within Irish and European literature – and, with regard to the efforts of Columbanus and others in the church, making an important contribution to the rebirth of European civilisation – the various groupings in Ireland continued their internecine warfare.

Although the Ulstermen's defeat at the battle of Moira may have ended their hopes of ever regaining mastery over the whole North, they nevertheless continued to resist Uí Néill expansion. The Ulaid suffered a severe defeat at Fochairt near Dundalk in 735, and it was possibly their alarm at Uí Néill encroachment upon the territory held by the Airgialla which explains why the Ulstermen fought alongside the latter at the battle of Leth Cam (near Armagh) in 827, in which the Uí Néill emerged victorious yet again, with many kings of the Airgialla being slain. Whatever autonomy had been retained by the Airgialla was now extinguished and their kings became mere vassals of the Uí Néill.

Despite these reverses, the Ulstermen continued to put up stubborn resistance, and in 1004 another great battle was fought at Cráeb Tulcha, in which the Cruthin king, the Ulaid king and many princes of Ulster were killed – indeed, complete disaster was possibly only averted because the victorious Uí Néill king was himself one of the fatalities. The *Annals of Ulster* recorded the event as follows:

The battle of Craebh-telcha, between the Ulidians and Cinel-Eoghain, where the Ulidians were defeated, and Eochaid, son of Ardgar, King of Ulidia, and Dubhtuinne his brother, and his two sons, viz. Cuduiligh and Domnall, were slain, and a havoc was made of the army besides, between good and bad, viz. Gairbhith, King of Uí-Echach, and Gilla Patraic son of Tomaltach, and Cumuscach son of Flathroe, and Dubhslanga son of Aedh, and Cathalan son of Etroch, and Conene son of Muirchertach, and the elect of the Ulidians besides. And the fighting extended to Dun-Echdach [Duneight, in the parish of Blaris], and to Druim-bó [Drumbo]. There also fell there Aedh, son of Domnall Ua Neill, King of Ailech, (and others, in the 29th year of his age, and the 10th year of [his] reign. But the Cinel-Eoghain say that he was killed by themselves. Donnchad Ua Loingsigh, King of Dal Araidhe, was treacherously killed by the Cinel-Eoghain.[67]

In 1099, another battle was fought between the same parties at the same place, where the invaders gained the day, and afterwards cut down the Cráeb, the sacred tree. Nevertheless, the continuing and determined resistance by the Ulstermen was a major obstacle to the Uí Néill gaining unchallenged control of Ulster, as Francis Byrne pointed out:

The Ulaid certainly were to remain for many generations a much more powerful force than later historians of the Uí Néill high-kingship cared to remember. ... In fact by the twelfth century, although the kings of Cenél nEógain were effective overlords of the North, the Ulaid were still struggling to preserve their independence. As long as their dynasty survived, in however attenuated a form, the Uí Néill could never call themselves kings of Ulster.[5]

With the Gaelic dynasties now the dominant political force within Ireland, it was only natural that their learned men and genealogists should seek to provide them with a lineage commensurate with their remarkable achievement. While engaged in such a task, the genealogists clearly felt the need to subsume those differences which existed between the Gaelic overlords and the more prominent sections of the pre-Gaelic population, though their attempts to do so have proven quite transparent to modern scholarship. As T F O'Rahilly remarked:

> In the early Christian centuries the ethnic origins of the different sections of the Irish population were vividly remembered, so much so that one of the chief aims of the early Irish historians and genealogists, was to efface these distinctions from the popular memory. This they did by inventing for the Irish people generally a common ancestor in the fictitious Míl of Spain. ... [They] were animated by the desire to invest the Goidelic occupation of Ireland with an antiquity to which it was entitled neither in fact nor in tradition; for only in this way would it be feasible to provide a Goidelic descent for tribes of non-Goidelic origin, and to unify the divergent ethnic elements in the country by tracing them back to a common ancestor.[22]

The pre-Gaelic peoples were each provided with lineages which linked them directly to the progenitors of the Gaels. One of the first to be so 'honoured' were the Cruthin, who were now claimed to be descended from one of Míl's sons, Ír.

> The invention of Ír was probably due in the first instance to the genealogists, who were favourably disposed towards the Cruthin and determined to provide them with a highly respectable Goidelic pedigree.[22]

111

This process of deliberate assimilation continued, with other important Irish dynasties being incorporated into the Milesian family tree, the number of Míl's sons eventually increasing to eight. However, as Francis Byrne pointed out: 'the mythological material is so rich and varied that not even the most assiduous monkish synchroniser nor the most diplomatic fabricator of pedigrees could bring complete order into this chaos. The resulting inconsistencies and anachronisms give us valuable clues.'[5]

Even without these determined efforts by the genealogists, Irish society was inevitably becoming more and more homogeneous. As the Celtic/Gaelic overlords would initially have been in a minority, their dominance could only have come about with the active assistance of the non-Celtic peoples who accepted their leadership. But another factor greatly assisted the process of homogenisation – the adoption of a new language.

Whether due to the influence, prestige or actual power of the Gaels, the language assumed to have been introduced by them became widely accepted among the population, certainly among the learned classes and within the developing Church. No doubt the mass of the population for a long time retained much of their own language or languages – references in ancient texts indicate that this was so – but these languages must inevitably have gone into decline, although with many loan-words – including Eriu, the ancient pre-Celtic name for Ireland, modern Éire – being incorporated into the new 'Irish' language, a language whose richness has made it a vital part of the cultural inheritance of the peoples of these islands.

New Invaders

The first recorded attacks by the Norsemen – the Vikings of popular imagery – occurred towards the end of the eighth century. In 795 they sacked the monastery of Iona; two years previously they had attacked the monastery of Lindisfarne on the east coast of Britain. Not that they had things completely their own way – in 811 they were defeated in a clash with the Ulaid. But still their depredations continued: in 823 they pillaged Bangor in a devastating assault during which it is said that 3,000 people died, manuscripts were destroyed and the monastery utterly wrecked. In 825 they raided Downpatrick and Movilla, but were badly beaten by the Ulaid.

These repeated attacks belatedly galvanised the Northern factions into concerted action. In 912, despite having recently been engaged in battle against each other, the Ulaid and the Uí Néill agreed a peace treaty, and when the Uí Néill next waged war on the Norse, they did so with the Ulaid in support, and the Ulaid king and the Uí Néill king fell together at the battle of Dublin in 919.

Notwithstanding the proven benefits of unified action, and despite the threat posed by the Norse incursions, internecine warfare among the Northerners eventually resumed, this time with the Norse drawn in as participants. In 933 Matudan mac Hugh of the Ulaid raided Monaghan with Norse allies but was routed by the Uí Néill (Matudan is commemorated in Ben Madigan, now Cave Hill, overlooking Belfast). In 942 the Norse raided Downpatrick, but were defeated after a pursuit by the Ulaid. The following year the Ulaid of Lecale exterminated the Norse of Strangford Lough. Yet, in 949, Matudan made the fatal mistake of plundering the Cruthin of Conailli Muirthemne in Louth, for the affront was avenged by the Iveagh Cruthin when they slew Matudan the following year.

Gradually, however, the early raiding of the Scandinavian invaders gave way to the establishment of permanent settlements, the development of trade and commerce, and the founding of such centres as Dublin, Wexford, Waterford, Wicklow, Cork and Limerick. The 'Vikings' gradually became assimilated into Irish society, and whatever bitterness the Irish felt about their coming was eventually relinquished. Which has not been the case with the next set of newcomers.

When, in 1169, the first of the 'Anglo-Normans' arrived on Irish soil, ironically they did so by invitation rather than invasion. They came at the request of Dermot Mac Murchada, deposed King of Munster, who sought their aid in a bid to regain his kingship. Although in popular perception these new arrivals are viewed as the first of the 'English', the roots of the initial contingents of adventurers and knights lay mainly in Wales and France, and many were 'Old British' in origin and far from being 'English' in either culture or ethnic background.

While the Irish might have greeted their arrival in Ireland with some suspicion and concern, the King of England viewed it with outright alarm. The last thing he needed was to have these freebooters and adventurers establishing power-bases so close to England's flank. He had little option but to react, and in that reaction he initiated the English Crown's long and troubled involvement with Ireland. But, as Lewis Warren pointed out, as far as the King of England was concerned Ireland was not a welcome acquisition, it was a nuisance.

King Henry II moved in. The Normans accepted his

overlordship, and so did the Irish kings. There was no campaign against the Irish. Henry II had no intention of conquering Ireland; he wanted to stop the Normans doing it. He made a treaty with the High King by which he was to have charge of the Normans and Rory was to mind the Irish. . . . In 1210 [Henry's successor] John mounted a major campaign in Ireland – not against the Irish, but against the Norman barons. The Irish cooperated with him; the king of Connaught sent his men to help John in the siege of Carrickfergus. . . . The leading families [among the barons] had Norman ancestors, but they had become as much a part of the fabric of society in Ireland as their descendants are today. Their counterparts among the Gaelic leaders imitated their lifestyle and adopted imported methods. They built castles, they issued charters, they had seals, they gave themselves coats of arms, they used the king of England's coinage. One of the demands was to have English law extended to the whole of Ireland. . . . [When later they tried to recover] lands from the settlers they were not recreating an Irish past. Many of them would have much preferred to become like English barons.[68]

The Earldom of Ulster

Henry II had established procurators to administer Ireland on his behalf. One of these, William FitzAudelin, seems to have had few positive attributes – Giraldus described him as 'a man full of guile, bland and deceitful, much given to wine and women, covetous of money and ambitious of Court favour' – but he was also overcautious and too ready to dampen the ardour of enterprising spirits such as John de Courcy, one of the adventurers who had accompanied him to Ireland.

But de Courcy was not to be restrained, and in 1177 he gathered around him some equally impetuous supporters and malcontents, then advanced boldly into Ulster, up until then unsullied by 'English' arms. With the element of surprise on his side he quickly captured Downpatrick, still the chief seat of the kings of Ulidia (the new name for Ulster), and the Ulidian King, Rory Mac Donleavy, had to precipitously flee. Within a week, however, Mac Donleavy had gathered a huge army and returned to confront the intruders, meeting de Courcy's much smaller forces on swampy ground just north of the town. In the battle which ensued the advantage possessed by Mac Donleavy's superior numbers was negated by the devastating impact of de Courcy's deadly crossbows, and the Ulstermen were defeated.

Although the following year de Courcy suffered two serious reverses, the internecine warfare so endemic in the North continued unabated, the Ulster leaders seemingly oblivious to the danger posed to them all by the enemy in their midst. From his stronghold in Downpatrick de Courcy carried the war into the surrounding districts, using to his advantage the inability of the Northern leaders to unite.

The Ulstermen, initially bitterly opposed to de Courcy's government, soon began to see it as offering some degree of protection against continuing attacks by the Uí Néill. In 1181 the Clan Owen 'gained a battle over the Ulidians, and over Uí Tuirtri, and over Fir-Li around Rory Mac Donleavy and Cumee O'Flynn.' Increasing raids by the Clan Owen in which they 'took many thousands of cows' forced the Ulidians to appeal to de Courcy for help. And so, when the Devlins and their kin again raided in 1182, they were met and defeated by de Courcy in alliance with the Ulidians. But there was a price to be paid, and this was to establish de Courcy ever more firmly in control of old Ulster.

What the Gaelic chieftains had attempted to do, but failed – effectively end Ulster's independence – was now to be accomplished by de Courcy, who installed himself as 'Master of Ulster' (princeps Ultoniae). Although he owed fealty to Henry II, this title was purely of de Courcy's own making and Mac Donleavy still officially remained 'Rex Ulidiae'. De Courcy's greatest achievements included the establishment of towns and ports and the building of two fine castles, at Carrickfergus and Dundrum. During this period a castle was also constructed where a sandbank created a ford across the River Lagan – present day Belfast. De Courcy reigned supreme in the territory he had won, and gradually opposition to his rule abated. He was especially benevolent to the Church, introducing Benedictine monks into Down and granting large tracts of land to others, besides endowing religious orders of various kinds.

John de Courcy's independent rule in Ulster aroused the jealousy of Hugh de Lacy, the English Crown's justiciar in Ireland, who misrepresented de Courcy to the new King John of England. As a consequence de Courcy fell into disfavour

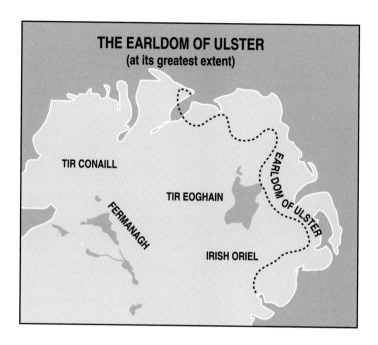

THE EARLDOM OF ULSTER
(at its greatest extent)

TIR CONAILL

TIR EOGHAIN

FERMANAGH

EARLDOM OF ULSTER

IRISH ORIEL

and was defeated by de Lacy at Downpatrick. Finally, on 29 May 1205 King John granted de Lacy all de Courcy's lands and created him Earl of Ulster. De Lacy and his half-brother Walter, however, soon showed John that he had mistaken his men, for by 1208 they were at war with the 'English of Munster' and proved more insubordinate than the Irish themselves. As T E McNeill pointed out:

> Judged as an attempt to make the whole of Ulster an English colony, the earldom was an outstanding failure, small in area and not very English. Within Ulster, however, it was a success; during the thirteenth century it dominated the whole of Ulster. John de Courcy raided far to the west in retaliation for raids from Tyrone, like any earlier Irish king. [69]

Extinction of Ancient Ulaid

On 24 June 1314 the Scots, under Robert the Bruce, defeated the English at the battle of Bannockburn. With this victory for Scottish independence Ireland's Gaelic chieftains, hoping to accomplish a similar overthrow of English authority, offered the kingship of Ireland to Robert's brother Edward, then 'Lord of Galloway'. Robert readily accepted, for the fierce ambition of his brother was a threat to the King of Scots himself. Hence, in May 1315 Edward Bruce landed at Larne on the Antrim coast, where he was joined by Robert Bisset with the Scots of Antrim and by Donald O'Neill of Tyrone.

The incumbent Earl of Ulster, Richard de Burgh, known as the 'Red Earl', had been in Galway at the time of Bruce's landing, and he immediately began to assemble a huge army to confront this threat. Bruce meanwhile overran Down and Louth, devastating old Ulster, destroying the 'English' there and their support.

Finally, both armies faced each other across the River Bann. De Burgh's was the larger, but one of his allies, Felim O'Conor of Connaught, was enticed by Bruce to desert the Red Earl. Confronted by this dramatic upset to the balance of forces Richard began to retreat, but was overtaken and forced to fight. The outcome of the ensuing engagement was the utter defeat of de Burgh, who lost the flower of his forces and fled south.

Bruce marched from victory to victory and was crowned King of Ireland on 1 May 1316, in the presence of a large assembly of Irish and Scottish nobles. His reign was to be short-lived, however, for he was finally defeated by an 'English' force under John de Birmingham near Dundalk in 1318. Edward was killed in the battle and with the death of this cruelly ambitious but exceptionally brave Lord of Galloway, the 'Scottish invasion' came to an end.

Bruce had brought with him some 6,000 Scottish mercenaries – the 'gallowglass' – and over the next few centuries it was these Scots, many of whom settled here, who proved vital to the resurgence of Gaelic Ireland.

However, the power of the Earls of Ulster had been crushed. The devastation in Ulster was followed by famine and this was soon accompanied by disease. All over Ulster the Anglo-Normans Gaelicised themselves to survive: the de Burghs adopted the name Burke, the de Mandevilles became the McQuillans, 'Lords of the Route' (Dalriada). With the destruction of Anglo-Norman power in the North the O'Neills now began to make claims to be known not merely as kings of Tyrone, their traditional title, but of the whole of Ulster. Prior to the collapse of the Earldom, as T E McNeill points out,

> They were never able to make this claim a reality of power or control, for a variety of reasons. Formally, they were forced constantly to admit that they had no right to it in English or Irish law. . . . For over 500 years it had been well known that Navan belonged to the Ulaid and . . . the Uí Neill dynasties had no claim to Ulster in the traditional sense. [69]

But now circumstances had radically changed, and a branch of the Uí Néill dynasty, known as the O'Neills of Clandeboye, planted themselves upon the ruins of the Earldom. A conquest begun many centuries earlier had finally reached its completion.

> It was therefore not until the end of the thirteenth century that the O'Neills could call themselves kings

of Ulster. And it was not until 1364 that the conservative *Annals of Ulster* can bring themselves to style Áedh Mór Ua Néill *rí Uladh*. Niall Ua Néill legitimised his claim in the eyes of the learned classes by holding a great feast for the poets of Ireland at the site of Emain Macha in 1381. The restoration of the name Ulster to cover once again the whole North was made possible only by the extinction of the kingdom of Ulaid.[5]

And with the extinction of ancient Ulster, Dalaradia, already largely subsumed within the Earldom, finally passed into history.

Postscript

The demise of Dalaradia did not, of course, mean the disappearance of its people. Their later history, however, has been dealt with in my other books – the primary objective here has been to focus on the history of the ancient kingdom of the Cruthin.

Ever since I first brought the Cruthin to the attention of a popular readership, and thereafter sought to promote the shared heritage of the Ulster people, an interesting, and at times quite heated, public debate has ensued. [Those readers wishing to know more I refer to Michael Hall's pamphlet *The Cruthin Controversy*,[70] in which he presents a comprehensive response to issues raised within that debate.]

Some critics claimed that my work was aimed solely at Ulster's Protestant community. Yet those who actually take the trouble to read my books – rather than rely on the misrepresentations penned by my detractors, or the unfortunate distortions indulged in by some of my supporters – will know that my purpose has never wavered, and remains as explicit as when I first enunciated it in the prologue to the first edition of *The Cruthin*:

> It is my purpose to trace these people to the present time and to give them back the history which has been denied them for so long, for they are the Ancient Kindred of Ireland as well as Britain. In doing so I hope that their origins will provide for them a basis of common identity rather than the cause of that running sore which is 'The war in Ireland'.[71]

If I was seemingly addressing only *one* section of our divided community, why would I talk of providing them with a *common* identity?

My hope is that this present book provides further evidence that the historical and cultural legacy of Dalaradia – a legacy which belongs in equal measure to *both* our communities (for, in essence, they are the *same* community) – was very much the product of a close interrelationship between *all* the peoples of the British Isles, using the term 'British' in its most ancient sense. Such an interrelationship is particularly evident in Dalaradia's rich literary output, a fact also noted by Seamus Heaney in the introduction to his translation of *Buile Suibhne*, when he said that 'it is possible . . . to dwell upon Sweeney's easy sense of cultural affinity with both western Scotland and southern Ireland as exemplary for all men and women in contemporary Ulster.'[72]

Despite the exclusiveness with which many in our community have defensively surrounded their respective traditions of 'Britishness' and 'Irishness', I take great encouragement from the efforts being made at the grassroots to explore the *commonality* of our historical and cultural heritage. In particular I note the work undertaken by the Farset Youth and Community Project, with which I have had a long association. Farset continues to involve young people from both sides of the 'divide' in an exploration of their *shared* inheritance – the sacrifice at the Battle of the Somme, the story of the *Titanic*, the idealism of United Irishman Jemmy Hope, the European dimension bequeathed us by Columbanus, the preservation of Ulster-Gaelic and Ulster-Scots, and many other equally significant facets.

Farset is appropriately sited to explore this inheritance, not simply because the citizens of Belfast are the predominant inheritors of ancient Dalaradia, but because its location provides ample evidence of the continuity I referred to at the beginning of this book.

Within the project's catchment area flows the river Farset from which the project takes its name. Close to the river once stood an old church, mentioned in a document of 1306 as the 'Ecclesia Alba', or White Church. The place name for this 'old church', *An tSeanchill*, first documented in the seventeenth century, has been Anglicised as 'Shankill'.

The old church has long since gone, but, as Richard S J Clarke noted, 'its graveyard continued to be used for burial for succeeding generations, maintaining a tradition established perhaps a thousand years earlier.'[73]   Three fragments from a 9th-century crozier were found in this graveyard and now reside in the National Museum in Dublin. These fragments, along with a bullaun stone also found in the graveyard (and now mounted near to the door of the adjoining St Matthew's Church) provide evidence of pre-Norman ecclesiastical activity.

Equally significant, the medieval parish of Shankill not only embraced the Falls as one of its native divisions, but was also directly linked to the monastery at Bangor. A church document of 1615 lists the chapel of Cromoge, located within the parish of Shankill, as one of six 'altarages', or parochial chapels, belonging to the monastery of Bangor, where oblations might be presented and dues paid.[74]

Tragically, to many people the words 'Shankill' and 'Falls' are synonymous with a deep-rooted communal division which some claim is unbridgeable. However, just as both districts were once embraced within one parish, it is my earnest hope that a proper exploration of our historical and cultural inheritance will reveal the full extent to which that inheritance has always been a *shared* one.

Appendix

William Reeves, in his *Ecclesiastical Antiquities*, made a list of entries in the ancient annals which referred to Dalaradia, explaining: 'The following notices, which are principally extracted from the Annals of the Four Masters [he indicates other sources by initials], shew that Dalaradia not only enjoyed a succession of chieftains from a very early date, but that it occupied a place of importance among the Irish principalities.'

[Inconsistencies in spelling are as in Reeves' original text. Entries in italics have been added to make his list more complete.]

AD 236   The Cruithne and Fiacha Araidhe defeated at the battle of Fothard Muirtheimne [in Louth] by Cormac O Coinn, King of Ireland. (*Tig.*)

AD 388   Milchuo, son of Hua Buain, King of North Dalaradia.

AD 478   Fiachra Lonn, King of Dalaradia, distinguished himself at the battle of Ocha, and received the territories of Lee and Cairloegh as a reward.

AD 555   Abbot Comgall of the Dál nAraidi founds Bangor monastic settlement.

AD 557   The battle of Mona-doire-lothair between the Cruithne and the Northern Hy-Niall; wherein Aodh Breac and seven lords of the Cruithne fell: after which Lee and Carn Eolarg were laid waste by the Hy-Niall.

AD 558   Aodh Dubh, son of Suibhne, King of Dalaraidhe.

AD 589   Columbanus sets off from Bangor on his great missionary journey to mainland Europe.

AD 615   Aedan, son of Mongan, King of Dalaraidhe, died. (*AU*)

AD 626   Fiachna, son of Baedan, King of Dalaraidhe, slain at the battle of Lethead Midhind in Drung. (*Tig.*) The *Four Masters* call him King of Uladh, adding that he fell by Fiachna Mac Demain, lord of Dal-Fiatach.

AD 637   Suibhne, son of Colman Cuar, son of Cobhthach, King of Dalaraidhe.

AD 637   *Decisive battle of Moira between Congal Cláen's Ulster forces and the Uí Néill leads to the Ulstermen's defeat and the end of any hopes they may have nourished of regaining control over the whole North. However, they still retain their independence in the east of Ulster for the next five hundred years.*

AD 665   Maolcaoich, son of Scandal, chief of the Cruithne of the race of Ir, died.

AD 680   Cathasagh, son of Maoldun, chief of the Cruithne, slain by the Britons at the battle of Rathmor of Moylinny.

AD 690   The Dalriadians spoiled the Cruithne and Ultonians. (AU)

AD 696   Aodh Aired, chief of Dalaradia, slain at Tulach-Garaisg in Farney.

AD 700   Fianan, son of O Dunchadha, King of Dalaraidhe, was strangled. (*Tig.*)

AD 706   Cucuarain, King of Cruithne and Uladh, was slain by Fionnchu O Renain.

AD 725   Battle of Murbholg between the Cruithne and Dalriadans.

AD 771   Battle between the Dalaraidhe at Sliabh Mis [Slemish], wherein was slain Nia, son of Cucongalta.

AD 778   Battle of Dumha Achidh between the Dalaraidhe, in which Focarta O Conalta was slain.

AD 787   Bresal, son of Flathrai, lord of Dalaraidhe, died. Tomoltagh, son of Innreachtach, King of Uladh, was slain by Eochaidh, son of Fiachna. (The *AU* at 789, and the *AI* at 776, represent Tomoltach, son of Innreachtach, as King of Dalaraidhe.)

AD 822   Eochaidh, son of Breasal, lord of Dalaraidhe-an-tuaisceirt [North Dalaradia] was slain by his own people.

AD 823   Maolbresail, son of Ailill Cobha, lord of Dalaraidhe, died.

AD 827   A victory obtained over the Danes by Lethlobhar, son of Longsegh. King of Dalaraidhe. (*AU*) (The *Four Masters* style him King of Uladh.)

AD 827   *Ulstermen fight alongisde the Airgialla at the battle of Leth Cam but are defeated by the Uí Néill.*

AD 831   Cionaedh, son of Ethach, lord of Dalaraidhe-an-tuaisceirt, was slain.

AD 847   Flannacan, son of Ethach, lord of Dalaraidhe-an-tuaisceirt, was slain by the Kinel-Owen.

AD 871   Lethlobhar, son of Longsegh, King of Uladh, died.

AD 892   Muredhach, son of Maoletigh, lord of Dalaraidhe, slain in battle at Rath-cro.

AD 896   Muredhach, son of Muretegh, King of Dalaraidhe, slain in battle. (*AU*)

AD 899   Muretegh, son of Lethlobhar, King of Dalaraidhe, died. (*AU*)

AD 904   Bec Ua Lethlobhair, lord of Dalaraidhe, died.

AD 912   Loingsegh Ua Lethlobhair, lord of Dalaraidhe, defeated at the Fregabhail by Niall, son of Aodh Finnliath, King of Ailech. His brother Flathrai Ua Lethlobhair fell in this battle. Another battle was fought between the same parties at Carn-Eirinn, where Loinsigh was again defeated.

AD 931   Loingsech Ua Lethlobhair, lord of Dalaradia, died. (*AU*)

AD 941   Ceallach, son of Bec, lord of Dalaraidhe, was slain in Oentribh [Antrim].

AD 960   An army was led by Flaithbhertach O Conchobhair, King of Ailech, into Dalaradia, which plundered the city of Connor.

AD 977   Lethlobhar Ua Fiachna, lord of Dalaraidhe, was slain.

AD 985   Flathri Ua Loingsigh, lord of Dalaraidhe, was slain by his own people.

AD 1003   Donnchadh Ua Loingsigh, lord of Dalaradia, and righ-damhna of Uladh, was slain by the Kinel-Owen.

AD 1004   Brian [Boroimhe], son of Cennetigh, marched with an army from Armagh to Dalaradia, and received hostages of the Dalaraidhe and Dalfiatach.

AD 1004   Battle fought at Cráeb Tulcha, in which many princes of Ulster are slain.

AD 1005   Brian, son of Cennetigh, proceeded with an army to exact hostages as far as Tirconnell and Tirone. Thence he passed across Fertais-camsa into Dalriada, Dalaradia, Ultonia, and Conallia Muirtheimhne.

AD 1015   A battle between the Ulidians and Dalaraidhe, in which the latter were defeated, and Domhnall, son of Loingsegh, their lord, was slain.

AD 1046   Conchobhar Ua Loingsigh, lord of Dalaraidhe, slain by the son of Domhnall Ua Loinsigh, in Leinster.

AD 1065   Domhnall Ua Loingsigh, lord of Dalaraidhe, slain by the people of O Meith.

AD 1070   Hua Eochaidhen, King of Dalaraidhe, slain by his own people. (AU)

AD 1077   Ua Loingsigh, lord of Dalaraidhe, slain by his own people.

AD 1095   A battle was fought at Ardachadh between the Dalaraidhe and Ulidians, in which the latter were defeated.

AD 1099   Second battle fought at Cráeb Tulcha, in which the Cráeb, the sacred tree, is destroyed.

AD 1113 Fionchas Ua Loingsigh, lord of Dalaraidhe, slain by Niall O Lochlain.

AD 1114 Donnchadh Ua Loingsigh, lord of Dalaraidhe, died.

AD 1130 Aodh Ua Loingsigh, lord of Dalaraidhe, slain in battle, in Ulidia.

AD 1141 Domhnall Ua Loingsigh, lord of Dalaraidhe, slain by the Cruithnigh.

AD 1156 Ua Loingsigh, lord of Dalaradia, slain by the Kinel-Owen.

AD 1158 Cuuladh, son of Deoradh Ua Flainn, lord of Hy-Tuirtre and Dalaraidhe.

AD 1177 John de Courcy slew Domhnall, son of Cathusagh, lord of Dalaradia.

AD 1189 Domhnall, son of Murtogh O Lochlain, killed by the English of Dalaraidhe.

AD 1198 The English of Moy Line and Dalaraidhe mustered 300 strong, and marched to Larne against Aodh O Neill.

AD 1364 *The Annals of Ulster for the first time style a member of the Uí Néill – Aedh Mór Ua Neill – as 'king of Ulster'.*

References

1   Lady Ferguson, *Sir Samuel Ferguson in the Ireland of his Day*, 1896.

2   Raoul Vaneigem, *The Revolution of Everyday Life*, Practical Paradise Publications, London, May 1975.

3   P A O Síocháin, *Ireland–A Journey into Lost Time*, Foilsiúcháin Eireann, Dublin.

4   H J Fleure, 'Prehistoric elements in our heritage', *Bull. John Rylands Lib.* 18, 1934.

5   Francis J Byrne, *Irish Kings and High-Kings*, Batsford, 1987, London.

6   E Estyn Evans, *Irish Heritage*, Dundalgan Press, 1942.

7   'Scene Around Six', UTV, 29.01.97.

8   *Irish News* 15.02.97.

9   W G Wood-Martin, *Traces of the Elder Faiths of Ireland*, Longmans, Green and Co., London, 1902.

10   E Estyn Evans, *The Personality of Ireland*, Blackstaff Press, Belfast, 1981.

11   Tomás Ó Fiaich, 'The Celts:1', in *The People of Ireland*, edited by Patrick Loughrey, Appletree Press/BBC, Belfast, 1988.

12   (Quoted by) Fanny Feehan, 'Suggested Links between Eastern and Celtic Music', in *The Celtic Consciousness*, edited by Robert O'Driscoll, The Dolmen Press, 1981.

13   Séan Ó Súilleabahadha and Reidar Christiansen, *The Types of the Irish Folktale*, 1963.

14   Tadhg Ó Murchadha, *Béaloideas*, XVIII, 30.

15   Bob Quinn, *Atlantean*, Quartet Books, London, 1986.

16   Kevin Danaher, 'Irish Folk Tradition and the Celtic Calendar', in

The Celtic Consciousness, edited by Robert O'Driscoll, The Dolmen Press, 1981.

17   Peter Woodman, 'Prehistoric Settlers', in *The People of Ireland*, edited by Patrick Loughrey, Appletree Press/BBC, Belfast, 1988.

18   Heinrich Wagner, 'Near Eastern and African Connections with the Celtic World', in *The Celtic Consciousness*, edited by Robert O'Driscoll, The Dolmen Press, 1981.

19   Charles Doherty, 'Ulster before the Normans: ancient myth and early history', *Ulster: an Illustrated History*, edited by C Brady, M O'Dowd & B Walker, Batsford, London, 1989.

20   Richard B Warner, 'Cultural Intrusions in the Early Iron Age: Some Notes', *Emania*, No 9, Belfast, 1991.

21   Francis J Byrne, 'Early Irish Society', *The Course of Irish History*, The Mercier Press/RTE, Cork, 1984.

22   T F O'Rahilly, *Early Irish History and Mythology*, Dublin Institute for Advanced Studies, 1984.

23   J P Mallory & T E McNeill, *The Archaeology of Ulster from Colonisation to Plantation*, The Institute of Irish Studies, Queen's University of Belfast, 1991.

24   Séan O Ríordáin, Antiquities of the Irish Countryside, Methuen, 1973.

25   Donnchadh Ó Corráin, 'Prehistoric and Early Christian Ireland', *The Oxford Illustrated History of Ireland*, edited by R F Foster, Oxford University Press, 1993.

26   Liam de Paor, 'The People of Ireland', *The People of Ireland*, edited by Patrick Loughrey, Appletree Press/BBC, Belfast, 1988.

27   Bishop McCarthy, quoted by Wentworth Huyshe in his edition of Adamnan's *Life of St Columba* (no date given).

28   W C Mackenzie, *The Races of Ireland and Scotland*, published by Alexander Gardner (no date).

29   Aiden Walsh, 'Excavating the Black Pig's Dyke', *Emania* 3, 1987.

30   Richard Warner, 'Tuathal Techtmar: A Myth or Ancient Literary Evidence for a Roman Invasion?', *Emania* 13, 1995.

31   *Silva Gadelica*, edited and translated by Standish Hayes O'Grady, Lemma Publishing Corporation, New York, 1970.

32   Rev H W Lett, 'The Great Wall of Ulidia', *Ulster Journal of Archaeology*, Vol III, No. 1, October, 1896.

33   R G Berry, 'The Royal Residence of Rathmore Moy-Line', *Ulster Journal of Archaeology*, Belfast, 1901.

34   Eleanor Hull, *Pagan Ireland*, David Nutt, London/M H Gill & Son, Dublin, 1904.

35   Charlie Doherty, 'The Problem of Patrick', *History Ireland*, Spring 1995.

36   *The Illustrated Road Book of Ireland*, The Automobile Association, 1970.

37   Tomás Cardinal Ó Fiaich, Archbishop of Armagh, 'Foreword' to *Bangor, Light of the World*, Ian Adamson, Pretani Press, Belfast, 1987.

38   Tomás Cardinal Ó Fiaich, 'The Beginnings of Christianity', *The Course of Irish History*, edited by T W Moody & F W Martin, RTE/The Mercier Press, Cork, 1984.

39   Adamnan, *Life of Saint Columba*, edited by William Reeves (1988 reprint from *The Historians of Scotland*, Edmondson and Douglas, 1874.

40   Murphy, *Early Irish Lyrics* (quoted in P Mac Cana; see reference 53).

41   J T Fowler, introduction to *Vita S. Columbae*, edited from Dr Reeves' text, Oxford, 1894.

42   Shirley Toulson, *Celtic Journeys*, Hutchinson, London, 1985.

43   Dumville, *Saint Patrick AD 493-1993*, Woodbridge. ON 1993.

44   Charles Thomas, *Britain and Ireland in Early Christian Times*, Thames and Hudson, London, 1984.

45   Richard Warner, *letter* to Ken Anderson, Ulster-Scots Language Society, 18.01.97.

46   W A Hanna, *Celtic Migrations*, Pretani Press, Belfast, 1985.

47   Daphne Brooke, *Wild Men and Holy Places: St Ninian, Whithorn and the Medieval Realm of Galloway*, Canongate Press, Edinburgh, 1994.]

48   Peter Hill, *Whithorn and St Ninian: The Excavation of a Monastic Town, 1984-91*, Stroud, 1997.

49   G S M Walker, *Works of St Columbanus*, Dublin, 1957.

50 *Joy of knowledge*, Guild Publishing, London, 1980.

51 Heinrich Zimmer, *The Irish Element in Mediaeval Culture*, 1891.

52 Duncan Norton-Taylor, *The Celts*, Time-Life Books, 1976.

53 Proinsias Mac Cana, 'Mongán Mac Fiachna and *Immram Brain*', *ÉRIU*, Vol. XXIII, edited by David Greene, Royal Irish Academy, Dublin, 1972.

54 Johannes Zschoke, J P Mallory, Hans G Eiken, Norman C Nevin, 'Phenylketonuria and the peoples of Northern Ireland', *Hum Genet*, 1997

55 Kay Muhr, 'The East Ulster Perspective on the Ulster Cycle Tales', *Emania* 14, 1996.

56 Douglas Hyde, *A Literary History of Ireland*, T Fisher Unwin, London, 1906.

57 Margaret E. Dobbs, 'The Dál Fiatach', *Ulster Journal of Archaeology*, Vol 8, 1945.

58 Richard Warner, contributor to *The Cruthin—A Common Culture?* BBC Radio Ulster, 12.07.89.

59 Compiled by Michael Hall from (1) *Táin Bo Cúalnge*, translated by Cecile O'Rahilly, Dublin Institute of Advanced Studies; (2) *The Táin*, translated by Thomas Kinsella, Dolmen Press, 1983.

60 Kuno Meyer and Alfred Nutt, *The Voyage of Bran, son of Febal, to the Land of the Living*, London, 1895.

61 *The Oxford Companion to Irish Literature*, edited by Robert Welsh, Oxford University Press, 1966.

62 *The Battle of Moira*, Samuel Ferguson, with historical introduction by Ian Adamson, Pretani Press, Belfast, 1980. Also *The Battle of Moira: an adaptation of Sir Samuel Ferguson's 'Congal'*, Michael Hall, Island Pamphlets: 10, Island Publications, 1995.

63 Elizabeth Healy, *Literary Tour of Ireland*, Wolfhound Press, Dublin, 1995.

64 *'Buile Suibhne': being The Adventures of Suibhne Geilt*, edited with translation, introduction, notes and glossary by J G O'Keeffe, published for the Irish Texts Society by David Nutt, London, 1913.

65 *The Mystic Dawn: Celtic Europe*, Fergus Fleming, Shahrukh Husain, C Scott Littleton and Linda A Malcor, 'Myth and the

Imagination of Mankind' series, Time-Life Books BV, Amsterdam, 1996.

66   *The Quest for Merlin*, Nikolai Tolstoy, Hamish Hamilton, London, 1985.

67   *Annals of Ulster*, edited, with a translation and notes, by William M Hennessy, HMSO, Dublin, 1887.

68   Lewis Warren, 'The Normans', in *The People of Ireland*, edited by Patrick Loughrey, Appletree Press/BBC, Belfast, 1988.

69   T E McNeill, 'Lordships and invasions: Ulster, 1177–1500', in *Ulster: An Illustrated History*, edited by Ciaran Brady, Mary O'Dowd and Brian Walker, Batsford, London, 1989.

70   Michael Hall, *The Cruthin Controversy*, Island Pamphlets No. 7, Island Publications, Belfast, 1994.

71   Ian Adamson, *The Cruthin*, Pretani Press, 1974.

72   Seamus Heaney, *Sweeney Astray*, Faber and Faber, London, 1984.

73   Richard S J Clarke, *Gravestone Inscriptions*, Ulster Historical Foundation, 1982.

74   Rev. Charles Scott, 'The Parish of Shankill', *Ulster Journal of Archaeology*, Vol.1, No.1, September 1894.

Index